I0803678

The Essence of Pairpoint

Fine Glassware

Marion and Sandra Frost

Schiffer Publishing Ltd
4880 Lower Valley Road, Atglen, PA 19310 USA

Unless otherwise credited, the photographs are of glassware in The Frost Collection.

Library of Congress Cataloging-in-Publication Data

Frost, Marion.
The essence of Pairpoint fine glassware/by Marion and Sandra Frost.
p. cm.
ISBN 0-7643-1419-X
1. Pairpoint Glass Works--Catalogs. 2. Glassware--United States--Collectors and collecting--Catalogs. 3. Tableware--United States--Collectors and collecting--Catalogs. I. Frost, Sandra. II. Title.
NK5198.P3 A4 2001
748.29144'85--dc21

2001001848

Copyright © 2001 by Marion & Sandra Frost

All rights reserved. No part of this work may be reproduced or used in any form or by any means—graphic, electronic, or mechanical, including photocopying or information storage and retrieval systems—without written permission from the copyright holder.

"Schiffer," "Schiffer Publishing Ltd. & Design," and the "Design of pen and inkwell" are registered trademarks of Schiffer Publishing Ltd.

Designed by "Sue"
Type set in Seagull Hv BT/Korinna BT

ISBN: 0-7643-1419-X
Printed in China
1 2 3 4

Published by Schiffer Publishing Ltd.
4880 Lower Valley Road
Atglen, PA 19310
Phone: (610) 593-1777; Fax: (610) 593-2002
E-mail: Schifferbk@aol.com
Please visit our web site catalog at **www.schifferbooks.com**
We are always looking for people to write books on new and related subjects. If you have an idea for a book, please contact us at the above address.

This book may be purchased from the publisher.
Include $3.95 for shipping. Please try your bookstore first.
You may write for a free catalog.

In Europe, Schiffer books are distributed by
Bushwood Books
6 Marksbury Ave. Kew Gardens
Surrey TW9 4JF England
Phone: 44 (0)20 8392-8585; Fax: 44 (0)20 8392-9876
E-mail: Bushwd@aol.com
Free postage in the UK. Europe: air mail at cost.
Please try your bookstore first.

We respectfully dedicate this book to the memory of the artisans of Pairpoint. May the continuing appreciation of your work stand as the ultimate testimonial to your creativity and craftsmanship.

Seems so odd that work can stay,
After hands have gone away.

Josephine Hintenach, 1937

Contents

Acknowledgments

During the two years that this long-contemplated book has been in development, there have been numerous people who have made individually unique and valuable contributions. We extend our appreciation and sincere gratitude to

Roberta Laufer, whose relentless prodding finally resulted in ink being applied to paper and whose threats of bodily harm hopefully prevented this work from being "just another picture book".

Ann Hintenach, our sister-in-law, who read and critiqued our first draft and offered valuable suggestions to improve its readability for the novice collector.

Charles and Barbara Coulter, who started out as dealer acquaintances and quickly became friends, for their hospitality when we visited New Bedford, Massachusetts, and their on-going generosity in providing us historical Pairpoint documents and artifacts. Thank you, Charlie, for plodding through a copy of the first draft and providing your experienced point of view.

Schiffer Publishing for being interested in publishing this work, and to Nancy Schiffer in particular for her guidance and assistance in making this book a reality. To Bruce Waters for his photographic assistance and creativity and to the fine Schiffer staff for their collective talents in making this book a work of art.

Preface

The study and collecting of fine glassware made by the Pairpoint Corporation of New Bedford, Massachusetts, has been one of the most satisfying and rewarding pastimes of our lives. As any of you who have developed a serious collecting interest know, the *plan* to start collecting *something* is rarely a deliberate one. Instead, it is the result of having *something* attract your attention. It is an emotional reaction that prompts one to want to learn more and become knowledgeable about a piece of the world around him. The desire for knowledge coupled with man's nature to horde has made *collecting* one of the most natural forms of entertainment. And so it was, and so it is, with us....

I was a furniture guy...the older the better. Dovetails were better than lobster tails. Hand planing and quality workmanship made my heart flutter. My wife liked glass...wasn't all glass Depression glass? Who could tell the difference anyway? I certainly couldn't, and, what's more, I could not have cared less! Dreadful stuff!

One day, about ten years ago, we stopped at Cathey's Antiques, on Route 301, in southern Maryland. We had been there before, so I knew I could look for furniture *in the rough* while Sandy looked at...ugh!...glass. When I had finished my tour of the back room, I waited impatiently, as guys do, near the front door, hoping that somehow this posturing would speed the wife up. While standing there, wondering how anyone could possibly spend so much time looking at glass, I felt something drawing my attention to the back corner of a display cabinet. "What manner of apparition goes here in southern Maryland?", I asked of no one. I turned to look, then walked closer, only to find the most beautiful form of glass I had ever seen...a tall green candlestick with hanging lustres. Directly above the gracefully proportioned, bell-shaped foot was a clear crystal ball containing a kazillion tiny air bubbles spiraling upward. "What kind of glass was this?", I thought. Sandy came over to see what could possibly have caught my attention in a display case, and she became smitten also. The tag said the candlestick was made by Pairpoint which, according to Sandy, was a maker of high quality glass. Well, we bought our first piece of Pairpoint glass that day, and it appears in its rightful position as the *numero uno* photograph in this book. We both knew then

NUMERO UNO, Pairpoint Candlestick #B-1811, with prisms, shown in green. This is the piece that started our collection.

that we had discovered "our" collecting niche, and today, ten years later, it has remained our pastime collecting passion.

Shortly after purchasing the green candlestick, we started looking for reference materials to learn more about the Pairpoint company. We discovered, at the public library, a copy of *The Pairpoint Glass Story*, by George C. Avila. This book made reference to The New Bedford Whaling Museum as a repository of examples of Pairpoint's product line. Sandy called the museum to seek more information about Pairpoint glass. She learned that a second book had been published in 1979, *Pairpoint Glass* by Leonard E. Padgett, and that he was a *neighbor* of ours in Maryland. Mr. Padgett was kind and most gracious when we contacted him; he had been similarly befriended and assisted by Orva Heissenbuttel, a noted journalist and authority on fine glass, when he began his Pairpoint collection. Ultimately, Len loaned us one of his personal copies of *Pairpoint Glass* and Orva befriended us on many occasions as she answered our questions and guided us patiently. Without the kindness, generosity, and patience of these two fine people, Sandy and I would probably never have achieved our current level of experience and interest in Pairpoint glass. Thanks to you both!

With the help of the books by Avila and Padgett, the personal guidance of Orva Heisenbuttel, and thousands of hours of searching and studying, we have amassed an extensive collection of Pairpoint glass products, as well as an intangible sense of the glass. We are not experts on the subject of Pairpoint glass; we don't know who could ever claim such a thing. But, we would like to share what we have learned with others. Our collection enables us to study in detail the shapes, patterns, and special characteristics. We point to examples from Pairpoint catalogs to verify many details. We describe in words those characteristics that cannot be shown in photographs to help you to develop a general *sense* of the glass.

This book is organized to be easy to use. The readers progress in a logical and orderly manner to identify Pairpoint products. By following the text and examining the examples closely through photographs, the reader can rule-out pieces that may have been thought to be from Pairpoint.

Although this book provides much of the technical *nuts and bolts* needed to recognize and identify Pairpoint glass, nothing can replace hands-on study. We encourage the collector to try to develop a *sense* of the glass by attending shows and asking questions. Hopefully this book will guide you in what to look for and how to *feel* the examples of Pairpoint glass you will encounter. As you progress in your Pairpoint glass education, the *sense* and *instinct* you will acquire will be at least as important, and possibly more so, than any of the identification technicalities we have provided in this book.

As with any reference material, this book is only as complete as the last tidbit of information can make it. It is a work-in-progress. We thank all the people who have helped us in the past and hope you will come to treasure Pairpoint glass as much as we do.

Marion and Sandra Frost
March, 2001

Introduction

How to Use this Book

During our years of collecting Pairpoint glass, we have learned that there is a logical procedure to follow when attempting to determine which company manufactured a particular piece of glass; we refer to this identification process as *attribution*. There are several elements almost always present that are considered during this process. Some elements have more importance than other elements, but all are needed to properly identify "who made what". To aid the collector, we have decided to divide this book into several categories according to what we consider to be their relative levels of importance. These primary categories would be: Shapes, Decorating Patterns, Colors, and Special Products. Although we recommend following the identification elements in the order that we have established, the collector may determine that the piece in question has an identification element unique enough to warrant starting at a different point in the book; or a collector may already recognize a shape and needs only to verify a pattern. Whatever the situation may be, it has been our goal to structure this book in such a way that each section operates independently from the others.

Shapes: *Learn Your Shapes!*

There is nothing more important than recognizing the many shapes made by Pairpoint. The shapes are very definitive as they represent the work at its most fundamental level. Colors can be changed and decorating designs of many types can be applied, but the shape, once conceived, is always constant. These *blanks*, as undecorated shapes are commonly known, may have had different destinations before they were offered to the general public for sale. After basic finishing operations such as grinding and polishing the pontil mark, the blank could have gone directly to the sales floor to be sold undecorated, or it could have gone into inventory to await transfer to Pairpoint's own cutting/engraving department. However, it is also possible that the basic blank could have been sold to a competitor or to an independent cutting/engraving shop to be decorated with their own designs. Therefore it is possible, although not particularly common, to find a Pairpoint blank decorated with a non-Pairpoint engraving pattern.

This raises a logical question regarding the attribution of any piece made by one company but decorated by another; who gets the credit? We can't give you an answer unless you want one that has "bias" written all over it. However, we can offer one observation that may help you decide. Every glass blank ever engraved by T.G.Hawkes & Co. was made by some other company (Corning/Steuben, Pairpoint, Heisey, etc.), but when discussed today, each of these products is attributed to "Hawkes".

This Pairpoint centerpiece bowl, Shape #A-106, has been engraved with an unknown, non-Pairpoint "Grape" pattern.

Opposite page:
This 8" Steuben Verre de Soie vase, Shape #2112, has been engraved and signed by T.G. Hawkes & Co. This item would normally be attributed as a Hawkes piece.

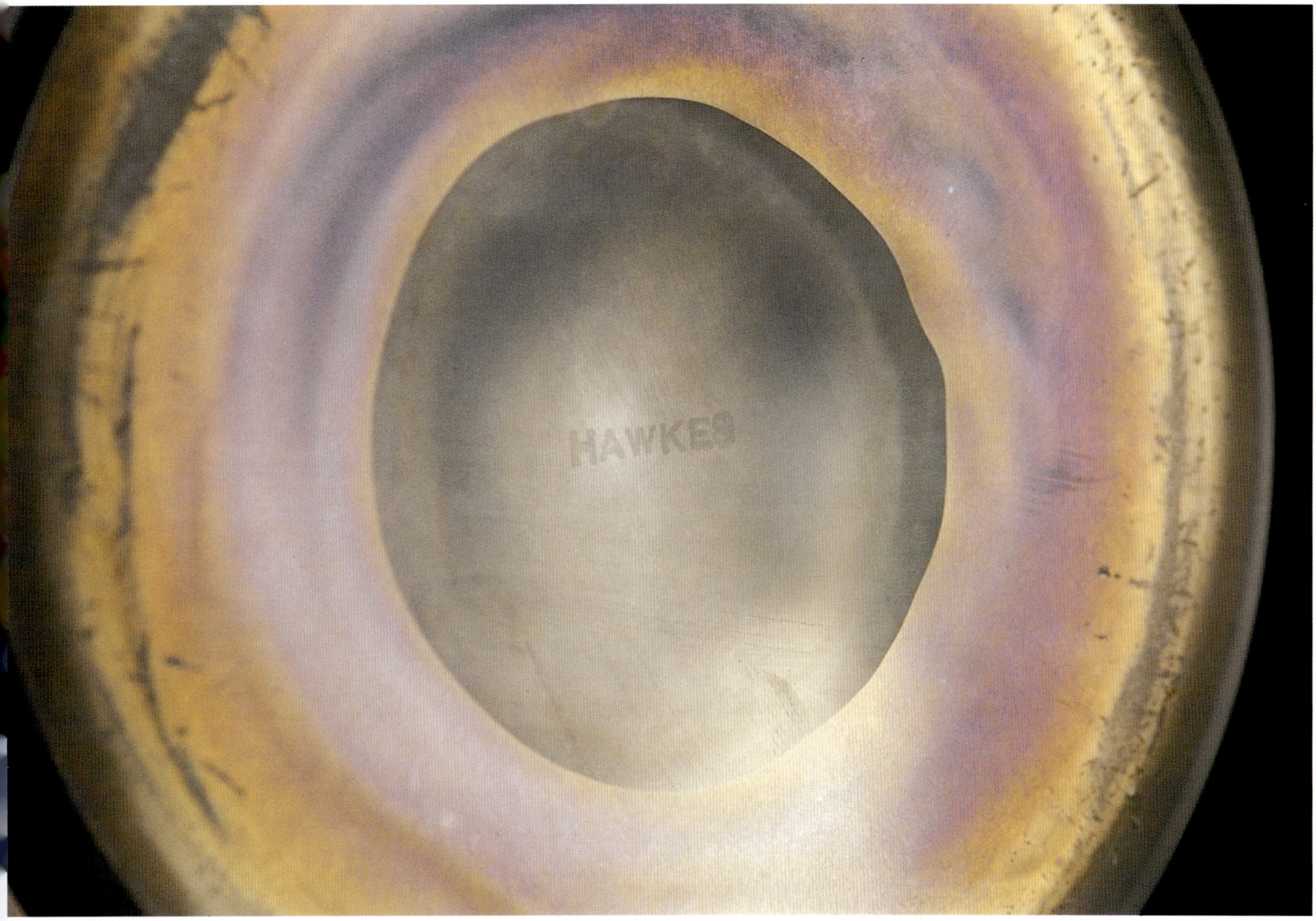

A view of the Hawkes signature applied by acid-etching to the Steuben vase in the adjoining photograph.

A comparison of two very similar shapes made by two different companies. The Steuben bowl on the left has an easily overlooked variation in the area where the foot is applied when compared to the Pairpoint bowl on the right. If you were not familiar with the slight color variation, and you didn't notice the variation in the foot, the Steuben bowl would easily be misidentified as Pairpoint. The diameters and heights are essentially the same. If you have the luxury of being able to compare the two items side by side, and you have keen powers of observation, the subtle variations are probably sufficient to detect the difference between the two bowls. Additionally, when viewed with a black light (as we have tried to demonstrate in the photograph), Steuben's Bristol Yellow does not fluoresce, while Pairpoint's Canarla does (observe the green tint on the top edge of the bowl).

Decorating Patterns

The knowledge that Pairpoint sold their blanks to other shops, whether through normal commerce or to help a competitor during periods of labor unrest or production shortages, or in the reverse where Pairpoint purchased blanks themselves, is significant when attempting to verify attribution. Just because you recognize a Pairpoint engraving pattern on an unidentifiable blank, you cannot conclude that the blank must have been made by Pairpoint. In this particular case, you will have relied upon your study of Pairpoint's patterns, not shapes, to develop the attribution. Similarly to find a known Fostoria blank, for example, that has a Pairpoint engraving pattern does not allow you to presume that Fostoria cut the exact same pattern as Pairpoint; many companies used similar designs, but the characteristics of each company's work is like a fingerprint. If you study the details of each design, you will eventually be able to discern the differences in style and workmanship.

Naturally the question from the preceding section comes up again. Would a Fostoria blank with Pairpoint engraving be a Fostoria piece or a Pairpoint piece? Or would it be more reasonable to attribute the piece as a "Fostoria blank with Pairpoint engraving"?

The most important thing to remember when one of the identifying elements is questionable is to not draw the conclusion that one element proves the other. In most cases you would be correct by default, but...misinformation tends to make one look foolish.

The section on *Decorating Pattern Motifs* has been included as a cross reference aid to those collectors or dealers that want a short-cut to attribution. By identifying a pattern or design characteristic, the reader is directed specifically to the various decorating patterns where that characteristic may be found. For example, if your piece has butterflies engraved, you will be directed to all of the Pairpoint patterns that include butterflies within the design. At best this section will have general application, but it may save searching through the book when time and/or patience is limited.

Colors

Of the primary identification categories, color would probably be the least useful in making a conclusive attribution. Many colors, including clear glass, of course, were generic to all glass manufacturers. However, within a color category, different hues and shades were used by different companies which render that color unique to a manufacturer. For example, we purchased a Steuben centerpiece bowl that, upon initial inspection, appeared identical to Pairpoint's A-194 centerpiece bowl. The size dimensions and the shape were the same. Essentially, the only difference was the color; it was not quite a Pairpoint color. In this instance we recognized the color as Steuben's Bristol Yellow. Further close inspection revealed an authentic faintly applied signature as well as some easily overlooked differences in the area of the foot. Without having knowledge of Steuben's design characteristics, absent the signature, and had the glass been clear, or some other generically used color, we would have incorrectly attributed the bowl to Pairpoint. Absolutely! So the point we are trying to make is that while color isn't necessarily a required identifying feature, it has the potential of being the final identifying feature.

Special Products

While colors alone may not be particularly helpful, special effects in shapes, color applications or patterns are self-attributing. All companies produced products of such a unique nature that identification is fairly clear-cut. Pairpoint was no exception to this fact. The use of color swirling in blanks, or special shapes, or special patterns in conjunction with certain shapes was commonplace for Pairpoint throughout the Middle Years of production. They did their best to demonstrate the incredible skills of their craftsmen while keeping up with current market trends. The study of these special items alone can direct your attribution without knowing your shapes first.

Values and Desirability

"What is it worth?" "Is it a good piece?" "How do I know if I'm paying a fair price?" How many times have you asked yourself these questions? (if only we had a nickel....). We know we've asked these questions over the years, especially in the early days of collecting Pairpoint glass. And, you know what?... no one really knew. Published reference materials, for all practical purposes, were unavailable and pricing guides were non-existent. Without knowing a piece was made by Pairpoint, many dealers would set their prices solely on the basis of their cost and their intuition as to the quality of the item.

During the preparation of this book, we knew the importance of providing the reader a reasonable idea of the value of the many items shown. We also knew that the establishment and inclusion of pricing guidelines could and probably would be the most contestable of all the information included in the book. We envisioned a serious dilemma. When we asked dealer friends what they thought our approach should be when setting pricing parameters, we received looks that approximated the facial expression caused by sucking on a lemon...no help there! So...we relied again on our own experience as we thought about comments made over the years by dealer friends, as well as our own perspective, as we have acquired or discussed other books that have come onto the market with pricing. Out of all the critical discussions and observations, two viewpoints clearly prevail. The first and most common viewpoint is that the author is using his book as a platform to *create* a market and artificially establish values that will ultimately serve his own interests. The second most commonly heard comment is far less devious in its purpose and that is the issue of inconsistent pricing. By mixing wholesale pricing, auction realizations, and show pricing, within one book, the reader gets a very distorted perspective of values. *Remember...values vary according to your position in the marketplace.*

We have attempted to avoid these criticisms by using pricing that is reasonably consistent with the most common venue where Pairpoint glass can be found. We believe that the pricing of Pairpoint glass at quality glass-oriented dealer shows, where knowledgeable buyers of reasonable means negotiate prices with experienced dealers of good repute, is the most consistently realistic indicator of fair market values. From this pricing perspective, discounting can be uniformly applied when conducting wholesale or liquidation transactions.

The methodology we used to establish price ranges for each item is partially objective in that we have observed dealer show pricing for many years, and partially subjective because of the many intangible factors that have to be considered. There exists great pricing inconsistencies in the marketplace that only serve to demonstrate the lack of familiarity that many dealers have with Pairpoint glass. Scarcity, artistry, visual appeal, execution of design, existence of engraving patterns, workmanship, attention to detail, color, and other factors contribute to a basic intrinsic value. This intrinsic value plays a major role in determining the market value of any specific piece of Pairpoint glass. The term we will be using to describe this collection of intangible factors is *DESIRABILITY*.

As you proceed through the upcoming design element chapters (Shapes & Blanks, Decorating Patterns, and Colors), you will see that we have provided price range and desirability information. When this information appears it relates specifically to the design element covered by the specific chapter you are reviewing. Whereas only the "Shapes & Blanks" chapter includes *Price Ranges*, only the "Decorating Patterns" and "Colors" chapters include *Desirability Factors* which we will refer to in the future as the *Score*. To properly value your specific item, you would first identify which *Shape* you have and note the *Price Range* for that shape. The next step would be to look into the "Decorating Patterns" chapter, if it applies, and the "Colors" chapter and *Score* your item according to the features that exist. By combining the *relative scores* of each of the two specified design elements into a *composite score*, you can then determine where within the specified *price range* your specific item falls. A *bottom score* of (1) would place the approximate value of your item at the bottom end of the price range, while a *perfect basic score* of (10) would place the value at the upper end. Any *intermediate score* would place the value somewhere proportionately within the price range.

Although a *perfect* composite score of (10) would indicate a Pairpoint shape made from the most desirable color of glass and engraved with the most beautifully designed and executed pattern, some items will come your way that have extra features. The use of two colors, or the application of a sterling silver overlay, or some other unusual characteristic will add a significant value surcharge to an otherwise normal inventory item. Therefore it is possible to have a unique piece that will score higher than (10). This will cause your Pairpoint item to be valued well above the price range indicated.

For your clarification and convenience, a step-by-step valuation worksheet is included at the end of this chapter. By following the simple procedure and adding any premium factors where they apply, we think that you will be able to establish a reasonable approximation of the retail value of your item. Also for further clarification, we have provided three sample worksheets displaying Pairpoint items that we have valued according to our valuation procedure.

When you get to the "Special Products" chapter, any pricing you find associated with a photograph, catalog reprint, or sketch will be for that particular item as it appears. This is because you won't find a multitude of design element combinations. Neither will you find a desirability factor because these pieces don't generally compare in an equal way with the general inventory items. The issues relating to scarcity and desirability will be addressed in the written text for each group of Special Products.

Always remember that when valuing an antique or collectible item, you are engaging in a very dynamic process. Unlike the price of a Chevrolet motor car being essentially the same wherever you shop for it, the ultimate purchase price of an example of Pairpoint glass could vary dramatically from one part of the country to another. The price will vary from show to show within the same geographical area and at different times of the year. So many things can affect the market price of Pairpoint glass that to commit pricing to print is at best an informed guess.

We think that Pairpoint glass has been grossly undervalued for a long time, especially when you take into consideration the high quality, the artistry, and its relative scarcity (we must see a hundred pieces of Steuben for every one piece of Pairpoint). Due to the lack of reference material and, therefore, the lack of public awareness, Pairpoint glass has generally not appreciated in value at the same rate as those products made by other comparable, but better documented, companies. We hope this book gives Pairpoint the public exposure it so badly needs and greatly deserves. Only then will the REAL market values emerge as you have informed quality-conscious buyers pursuing an ever-decreasing supply of some of the finest glass made in the world!

VALUATION WORKSHEET

A Step-by-Step Guide to Valuing Your Pairpoint Treasure

ITEM: ______________________	DESCRIBE FEATURE	ENTER SCORE	PRICE RANGE
1. Identify your *Shape* in the Shapes and Blanks chapter and record the size and price range.	________		$________
2. Identify your *Decorating Pattern* and record the desirability score. If your item is undecorated, enter a zero.	________	______	
3a. Identify the primary *Color* of your item and record the desirability score for that color.	________	______	
TOTAL YOUR BASIC SCORE:		______	Perfect Score = 10
3b. Identify the *second Color* of your item, if applicable, and record the desirability score for that color. (A clear bubble ball connector or base does not qualify as a second color).	________	______	
3c. If your item has a bubble ball connector or base or a hollow ball connector that is made of *colored* glass, record that color's score.	________	______	
4. If your item has a *hollow ball connector* that is *engraved*, enter a score of (5).	________	______	
5. If your item has *prisms*, enter a score of (3).	________	______	
6. If your item is of two colors, and those colors are *Flambeau and Black Amethyst*, enter a score of (5).	________	______	
7. If your item is cased glass with the *color cut-to-clear*, enter a score of (10).	________	______	
8. If your item is decorated by *silver overlay or applied silver enameling*, enter a score of (10).	________	______	
FINAL SCORE AND VALUE:		______	$________

(For scores exceeding (10), increase the highest value in the price range recorded in Step 1 by the same proportion that the final score exceeds (10).

VALUATION WORKSHEET
A Step-by-Step Guide to Valuing Your Pairpoint Treasure

ITEM: #1600 Candlestick	DESCRIBE FEATURE	ENTER SCORE	PRICE RANGE
1. Identify your *Shape* in the Shapes and Blanks chapter and record the size and price range.	10 3/4"		$ 175-400
2. Identify your *Decorating Pattern* and record the desirability score. If your item is undecorated, enter a zero.	Grapes	5	
3a. Identify the primary *Color* of your item and record the desirability score for that color.	Cobalt Blue	5	
TOTAL YOUR BASIC SCORE:		10	Perfect Score = 10
3b. Identify the *second Color* of your item, if applicable, and record the desirability score for that color. (A clear bubble ball connector or base does not qualify as a second color).	N/A		
3c. If your item has a bubble ball connector or base or a hollow ball connector that is made of *colored* glass, record that color's score.	N/A		
4. If your item has a *hollow ball connector* that is *engraved*, enter a score of (5).	N/A		
5. If your item has *prisms*, enter a score of (3).	N/A		
6. If your item is of two colors, and those colors are *Flambeau and Black Amethyst*, enter a score of (5).	N/A		
7. If your item is cased glass with the *color cut-to-clear*, enter a score of (10).	N/A		
8. If your item is decorated by *silver overlay or applied silver enameling*, enter a score of (10).	N/A		
FINAL SCORE AND VALUE:		10	$ 400

(For scores exceeding (10), increase the highest value in the price range recorded in Step 1 by the same proportion that the final score exceeds (10).

VALUATION EXAMPLE #1: Pairpoint #1600 Candlestick, 10.75" high, Cobalt Blue, Engraved "GRAPES".

VALUATION WORKSHEET
A Step-by-Step Guide to Valuing Your Pairpoint Treasure

ITEM: #B-366 Comport

	DESCRIBE FEATURE	**ENTER SCORE**	**PRICE RANGE**
1. Identify your *Shape* in the Shapes and Blanks chapter and record the size and price range.	8" dia		$175-400
2. Identify your *Decorating Pattern* and record the desirability score. If your item is undecorated, enter a zero.	NONE	0	
3a. Identify the primary *Color* of your item and record the desirability score for that color.	Green	3	
TOTAL YOUR BASIC SCORE:		3	Perfect Score = 10
3b. Identify the *second Color* of your item, if applicable, and record the desirability score for that color. (A clear bubble ball connector or base does not qualify as a second color).	N/A		
3c. If your item has a bubble ball connector or base or a hollow ball connector that is made of *colored* glass, record that color's score.	N/A		TOTAL SCORE = 3 ÷ PERFECT SCORE = 10 } 3/10
4. If your item has a *hollow ball connector* that is *engraved*, enter a score of (5).	N/A		
5. If your item has *prisms*, enter a score of (3).	N/A		Price Range Variation 400 − 175 = $225
6. If your item is of two colors, and those colors are *Flambeau and Black Amethyst*, enter a score of (5).	N/A		3/10 of the Variation = $68
7. If your item is cased glass with the *color cut-to-clear*, enter a score of (10).	N/A		Bottom Value = $175 + 3/10 Variation = 68
8. If your item is decorated by *silver overlay or applied silver enameling*, enter a score of (10).	N/A		VALUE EST → $243
FINAL SCORE AND VALUE:		3	$ 243

(For scores exceeding (10), increase the highest value in the price range recorded in Step 1 by the same proportion that the final score exceeds (10).)

VALUATION EXAMPLE #2: Pairpoint #B-366 Comport, 8" diameter x 7.25" high, Green, Not Decorated.

VALUATION WORKSHEET
A Step-by-Step Guide to Valuing Your Pairpoint Treasure

ITEM: #B-1485 Vase

	DESCRIBE FEATURE	ENTER SCORE	PRICE RANGE
1. Identify your *Shape* in the Shapes and Blanks chapter and record the size and price range.	13"h		$225-650
2. Identify your *Decorating Pattern* and record the desirability score. If your item is undecorated, enter a zero.	NONE	0	
3a. Identify the primary *Color* of your item and record the desirability score for that color.	Flambeau	5	
TOTAL YOUR BASIC SCORE:		5	Perfect Score = 10
3b. Identify the *second Color* of your item, if applicable, and record the desirability score for that color. (A clear bubble ball connector or base does not qualify as a second color).	BLACK AMETHYST	5	
3c. If your item has a bubble ball connector or base or a hollow ball connector that is made of *colored* glass, record that color's score.	N/A		
4. If your item has a *hollow ball connector* that is *engraved*, enter a score of (5).	N/A		
5. If your item has *prisms*, enter a score of (3).	N/A		
6. If your item is of two colors, and those colors are *Flambeau and Black Amethyst*, enter a score of (5).	Yes	5	
7. If your item is cased glass with the *color cut-to-clear*, enter a score of (10).	N/A		
8. If your item is decorated by *silver overlay or applied silver enameling*, enter a score of (10).	Yes	10	
FINAL SCORE AND VALUE:		25	$ 1,625

A final score of 25 is 2½ times the perfect score of 10.

Multiply the top value of the price range, which represents a score of 10, by 2.5.

$650
x 2.5
$1,625

(For scores exceeding (10), increase the highest value in the price range recorded in Step 1 by the same proportion that the final score exceeds (10).)

VALUATION EXAMPLE #3: Pairpoint #B-1485 Vase, 13.25" high, Flambeau body with Black Amethyst Foot, Sterling Silver Overlay.

Condition

We don't think we are letting you in on any big secret when we say that condition is probably the single most important factor when it comes to placing a monetary value on a collectible item. Glass is certainly no exception to this fact, but due to the many ways a piece of fine hand-worked glass can be compromised, it is worth exploring the issue further.

We believe that the condition issues involved when deciding whether or not to purchase a piece of Pairpoint glass and what price to pay are multi-faceted and often very personal. Due to the subjective nature of evaluating condition, we can't tell you what flaw or damage is acceptable; we can only suggest things to think about as you are making your decision. The different issues we discuss below represent our own personal point of view and are the thoughts that guide us in our search for Pairpoint glass; our point of view may not work for you. That is for you to decide.

If you take the time to read thoroughly the various sections of this book and become familiar with those features and conditions that are supposed to exist, your ability to detect a flaw or aberration in an example of Pairpoint glass should become well-honed. Look the piece over carefully and thoroughly with both your eyes and your fingers; hold it up to the light. Don't skim over the piece; look at it section-by-section, and inch-by-inch. Take your time!

An example of edge grinding to remove a chip. This photo shows an unusually poor attempt at improving (?) the look of this Pairpoint #B-1485 Vase. Most edge grinding will be of better quality, but this example really shows the destruction involved.

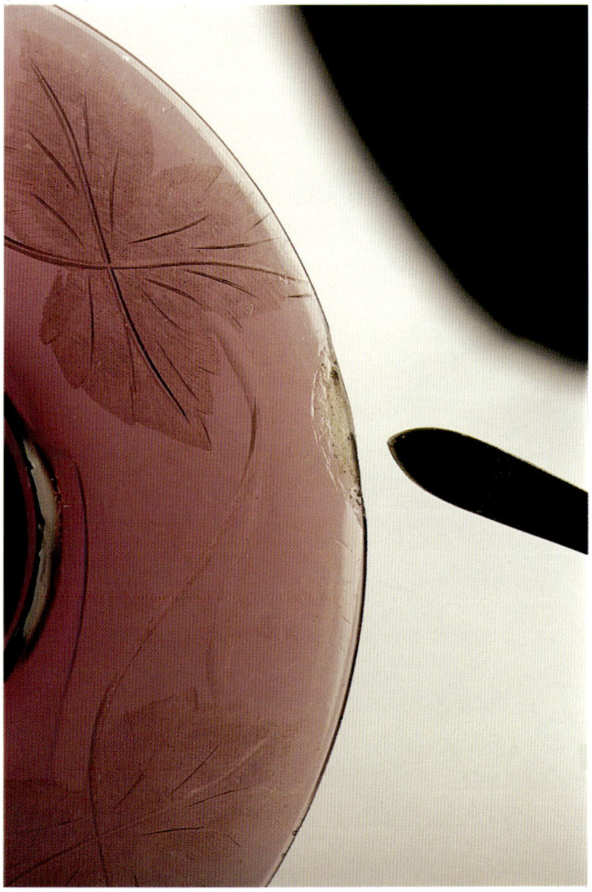

This photograph shows a chip that has been made less obvious by the application of a tinted resin compound. The adjacent glass has neither been ground nor altered in any way, and the process is reversible. This type of "repair" helps to make the item serviceable although the value remains diminished.

Chips

There are big chips called *chunks*, medium chips called *chips*, flat chips called *flakes*, small chips called *bruises*, tiny chips called *flea bites*, and extremely tiny chips called *roughness*. The different terms we use seem to help us cope with the fact, and minimize the harsh reality, that our potential sale or purchase is damaged to some degree. For all practical purposes, the existence of a chip greatly diminishes the value of the item and renders it hard to sell. If you are a tolerant buyer and can negotiate a lowered price and only want to use the piece as a decorative item in your home, chips of the smaller variety may be acceptable. If you think you may want to resell the item sometime in the future, say your sad farewell, lament the damage to a fine work of art, and move along.

Ground Edges

This is the procedure used when someone can't cope with a chip. It is the deliberate grinding away of the chip in a cosmetically uniform way. In other words it is the destruction of all the surrounding area in such a way that the chip no longer exists as a chip. It is the most common way today that chips are made to *disappear*. In our opinion there is *good* grinding and there is *bad* grinding, and we are not referring to the skill level of the glass repairman. We are referring to the purpose that gives rise to the decision to grind a chip out of a piece of glass. If you have rim chips on some of the wine glasses your grandmother left you in her will, and you want to be able to use the glasses for special occasions without having to administer first aid afterwards, by all means have the glasses repaired; this is *good* grinding. However, if you repair by grinding an item that will be offered for sale and don't acknowledge the repair or properly adjust the price to reflect the repair, then a fraud has been perpetrated; this is *bad* grinding.

We believe in letting a fine glass object with a chip remain *honest*. If the piece is scarce or unusual, we would consider the purchase. There are resins available that can be used to fill the chip, making the piece usable, without destroying the original lines and integrity of the piece. It would be a rare circumstance that we would knowingly purchase a piece of Pairpoint glass that has been cosmetically altered by grinding.

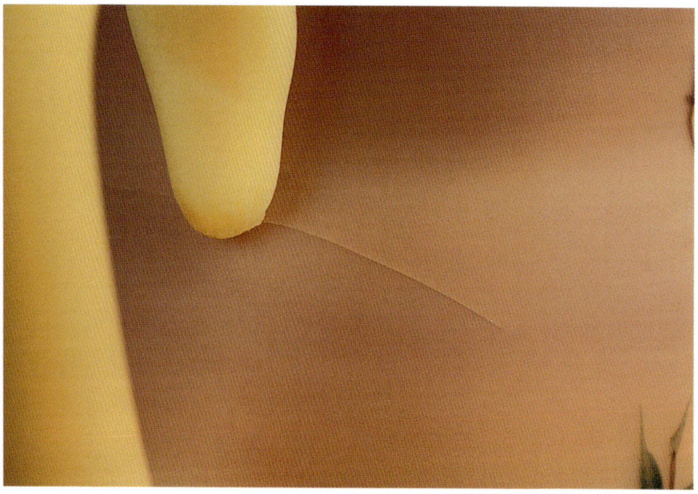

An example of a "heat check", or crack, that occurred during the manufacturing process. We believe that uneven stresses were created at the time the handle was applied to this decorated Gundersen Burmese pitcher and the crack appeared during the cooling process. Because this item was (1) scarce and desirable, (2) very cheap, and (3) unlikely to crack further, we decided it would make a nice shelf-display item within our collection.

Cracks

Occasionally you will come upon an item that has an internal stress crack which was most likely caused by the uneven equalization of forces within the item as it cooled after production. It is also possible for an internal crack to occur as a result of careless handling such as rapid temperature changes caused by too high or too low of a water temperature when washing the item. Internal cracks may be acceptable under certain conditions such as a very low purchase price, or the cracked piece is free if you purchase the paired mate at a normal price, or if the crack is hard to see and doesn't appear that it will spread. As a general rule however, stay away from items with cracks.

This is an example of a crack that we believe was the result of improper handling. Because there is no chip at the very edge of the bobeche, and the crack stops a little before reaching the edge, we think hot candle wax, or a short candle, probably introduced a concentration of heat in this one area. We would never have purchased this candlestick had it not been one of a pair with a price tag that reflected the value of a single stick.

Factory Defects & Toolmarks

Within any hand-worked item, it is possible to find an occasional air bubble, a dirt speck, a heat check (crack), a glass drip, or tooling marks. Each flaw should be evaluated on its own merit. Depending upon the nature of the flaw, the price of the item may or may not be affected adversely. This is really a judgment call on the part of the buyer.

A Note of Interest: It was very common for glass companies to specifically send their blanks containing flaws to the engraving/cutting department where those flaws would be *ground-out* as the design was *ground-in*.

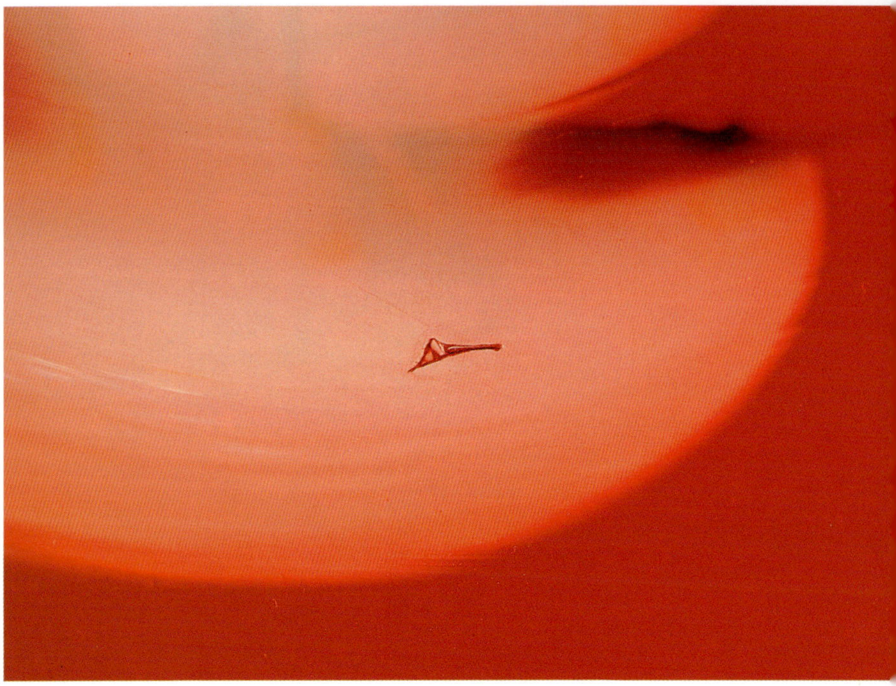

This photograph shows an errant splatter of molten glass that somehow landed upon the interior surface of a very scarce Gundersen bowl. The flaw is small but is readily discernible. Our decision to purchase this bowl was twofold. The item was very inexpensive, and it allowed us to fill-out a three-piece console set that, considering the scarcity of the form, we never thought would happen.

Leaning & Crookedness

"There was a crooked man who...lived...in a little crooked house." Sometimes crookedness just happens, even with Pairpoint glass. A stem will be bent, a rim may droop, or a bowl may sit slightly misaligned on its base. You would be amazed at how common crookedness and wobbliness is; it's usually just a matter of degree. From our perspective (please don't ask us why we have a perspective), crookedness can be the hardest defect to notice. So...get into the habit of rotating each item while it sits on a table or shelf and observe the motion that results; hopefully it will be minimal. Major bends, crookedness, or out-of-rounds would not be a good thing...leave it behind.

Our admission as to why we have a perspective on leaning and crookedness. When we purchased this very hard-to-find Flambeau and Black Amethyst comport with sterling silver overlay, we really looked it over for flaws. The only thing we did NOT do was to rotate it in place on the table top. Oh, well..."you pays your money, and you takes your chances".

A comparison between two examples of Pairpoint's Tavern Glass vases. The vase on the left is normal, while the vase on the right is *sick* (cloudy). This condition may appear all over, or it may appear in ringed bands around the circumference where water levels may have been over the years.

Cloudiness (Sickness)

This is the condition where the interior surface of, most usually, a vase or bowl has been finely etched and has a permanent milky-white appearance. This is the result of years of use during which time water was allowed to sit and evaporate over an extended period of time without the benefit of frequent washing and drying. Unfortunately this condition is far too common and greatly reduces the value of the item.

When examining an item that appears *dirty*, don't automatically assume that the glass just needs a good cleaning to return it to its sparkling beauty. Wet your finger or a tissue and rub an area to see if the area comes clean; if it is dirt, it will. But, if the area returns to an opaque, hazy appearance after the wetness has dried, then the glass is *sick*. *Be very observant because surface dirt will hide permanent cloudiness*.

There is good news, however. In most cases the cloudiness can be permanently removed by mechanical polishing. There are a few companies around that can bring your sick glass back to life at a very reasonable and affordable cost. (Refer to the *Support Services* chapter for our recommendation.) The proprietary techniques they use are legitimate and very effective; the only negative is that the process is slow. Your item may be gone for a couple months, but the wait is worthwhile. In order for this technique to work, the sick area must be open and accessible so that the polishing compounds can be inserted and removed. We have seen some Pairpoint items with hollow, but totally enclosed, stems that have had an internal cloudiness caused at the time of manufacture; these pieces would not lend themselves to restoration.

A Word of Caution: There are liquid compounds offered on the market that claim the ability to make your sick glass look good again. These products are little more than temporary wetting agents that do not repair the condition, only disguise it. Be careful when thinking of purchasing an item that someone hasn't used one of these wetting agents to make the item appear healthy. A giveaway could be the existence of an oiliness on the interior surface of the item.

This Pairpoint #B-1107 Vase, shown in Marina Blue, was so cloudy that when you placed your hand inside, you could not see anything but a shadow through the glass. What is shown in this photograph is the end result of having the vase *cleaned* by Kim Carlisle and Associates. I believe the process cost us $35.00, about two years ago.

A Pairpoint Bowl, shown in Cobalt Blue, which displays the brass connector between the bubble ball and the top of the foot.

A closer view of the brass connector shown in the adjoining photograph.

Repairs

This is perhaps a somewhat redundant and possibly contradictory paragraph, because we have just spent time discussing issues relating to the ways glass can be altered and repaired. Except for the cleaning of cloudy glass, it is hard to imagine any repair achieving any reasonable standard of quality. However, we have seen one technique that we think is a repair, but can't say with any degree of certainty. Seven or eight years ago, we purchased a cobalt blue centerpiece bowl that utilized the bubble ball connector as part of the stem configuration. Beneath and partially cradling the bubble ball was a machine-formed brass connector that transitioned perfectly into the domed foot of the bowl. The quality, shape, and fit of the piece was *right* and actually duplicated the stem area as if it were the normal glass form. Our initial thought went something like this: *Hubby broke Wifey's cherished bowl while she was visiting her Aunt Ruth in Seattle. Having the good fortune of being a machinist by trade, he rushed to his basement workshop and fabricated this connector on his lathe. Once assembled, he was sure his wife would never notice the difference. (Some guys really do think that way!)* We were certain that we had come upon an out-of-the-blue high quality repair. But, about two years later in a totally different geographical area, we came upon a cobalt blue vase with a perfectly styled and beautifully executed brass connector. Like the bowl we found, the connector was in the stem area, but this time it connected the top of the bubble ball to the bottom of the upper vase. With the connector in place, the vase retained the same height as if the vase were all glass. Now...we had to ask ourselves, "What are the chances that *Hubby* broke an-

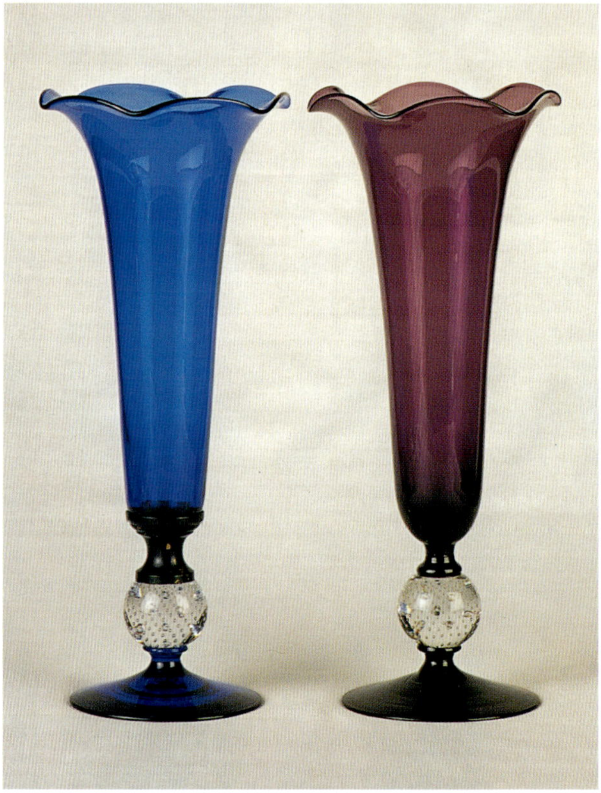

A comparative example of two Pairpoint #B-960 Vases. The cobalt blue vase on the left has a black-painted brass connector between the bowl of the vase and the top of the bubble ball, and the amethyst vase on the right is *normal*. Notice that the heights are the same and the connector blends in very well with the overall design.

other one of *Wifey's* prizes in exactly the same way?"...not very likely!

We really don't quite know what to make of this aberration. After giving much thought to every conceivable scenario, we reoriented our thinking to consider a very basic question. With the glass thickness and obvious strength of the stem areas on both of our examples, how would they have broken in half? Had they been mishandled or knocked over, surely the foot or rim would have taken the brunt of any impact and would have broken or cracked first; this was not the case with either piece. Until we discover authoritative information that addresses this curiosity, we are left to ponder the following three possibilities:

1.) The metal connectors were intentionally included as part of the design. Pairpoint did extensive metal fabrication for their Fine Arts Line and had the means to easily fabricate these parts. However, since the connectors don't really add anything significant to the overall design, "Why bother?".....or

2.) Pairpoint could have provided a factory repair service for customers that had damaged either the upper or lower portion of one of their products. The damaged portion could have been totally cut away and a newly-fabricated section added through the use of a perfectly styled metal connector. To us, this seems like a lot of trouble and expense to salvage an item that cost $10-15 new in the 1920s....or

3.) An enterprising person could have made connectors on speculation waiting for the world to beat a path to his door so that they could repair all of their Pairpoint items that had broken in exactly the same way. The problem with this possibility, other than the reliance on a lot of coincidence, is that the shape and dimension of each hand-made Pairpoint item was different; there would have been no chance that a pre-made metal connector would have universally mated with items broken at random.

We leave the solution to this dilemma to you; the burden is squarely upon your shoulders. Anyone knowing more about these metal connectors is asked to contact the authors.

A Final Word About Condition

When evaluating adverse conditions on a piece of glass you are thinking of purchasing, it is imperative that you keep one concept in mind. As you search for Pairpoint glass, you are searching for items that are becoming very hard to find in general, and within the Pairpoint product line there are a number of items that are particularly scarce. The likelihood of ever seeing some of these items is very remote. Therefore, as with any object of great rarity, don't cast it off too readily just because it may have some damage; you may never find another example. Even damaged examples of scarce art objects retain value.

This Mt. Washington Lava/Iris Iridescent Glass Oil Lamp is extremely scarce and valuable. However, it has been professionally repaired in the neck area where there had been a fracture. To have discarded this item because it was damaged would have been a travesty; the nominal cost to effect a high quality repair was more than justified.

Chapter 1.

Historical Pondering

Over the last thirty years, the history of the Pairpoint Corporation and its predecessors has been chronicled by well-respected authors and students of Pairpoint Glass. The evolution of the company was typical of many industrial enterprises of its time, taking many forms and courses as it moved forward through history. The *nuts and bolts* of this evolution has been documented frequently enough that we are not going to do the same here; the facts are confusing and, though not irrelevant, don't really fulfill the purpose of this book. Instead, an accounting of the basic history, an understanding of the social and economic factors affecting public taste, and a comprehensive look at the characteristics of the glass itself will better enable the reader to develop a real *sense* of the glass.

The carbon copy of an original letter written by Robert Gundersen to Mr. William Elsholz in response to Mr Elsholz's request for historical information about the Pairpoint Glass Companies. This letter was salvaged from the abandoned Pairpoint factory in New Bedford, Massachusetts, during the early 1960s, by Charles Coulter. *Courtesy of Charles and Barbara Coulter.*

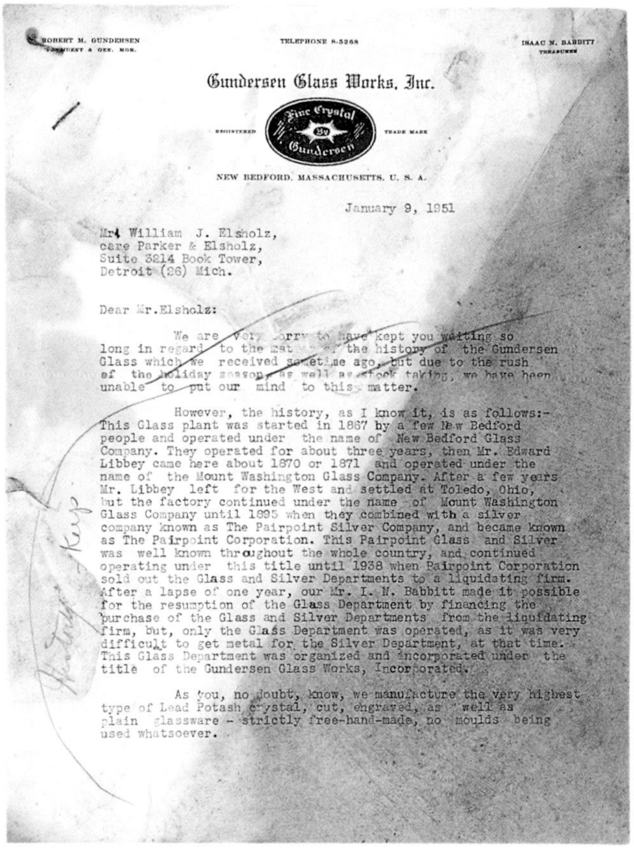

ROBERT M. GUNDERSEN TELEPHONE 8-5268 ISAAC N. BABBITT

Gundersen Glass Works, Inc.

Fine Crystal By Gundersen

REGISTERED TRADE MARK

NEW BEDFORD, MASSACHUSETTS, U. S. A.

January 9, 1951

Mr. William J. Elsholz,
care Parker & Elsholz,
Suite 3214 Book Tower,
Detroit (26) Mich.

Dear Mr. Elsholz:

We are very sorry to have kept you waiting so long in regard to the matter of the history of the Gundersen Glass which we received sometime ago, but due to the rush of the holiday season, as well as stock taking, we have been unable to put our mind to this matter.

However, the history, as I know it, is as follows:- This Glass plant was started in 1867 by a few New Bedford people and operated under the name of New Bedford Glass Company. They operated for about three years, then Mr. Edward Libbey came here about 1870 or 1871 and operated under the name of the Mount Washington Glass Company. After a few years Mr. Libbey left for the West and settled at Toledo, Ohio, but the factory continued under the name of Mount Washington Glass Company until 1895 when they combined with a silver company known as The Pairpoint Silver Company, and became known as The Pairpoint Corporation. This Pairpoint Glass and Silver was well known throughout the whole country, and continued operating under this title until 1938 when Pairpoint Corporation sold out the Glass and Silver Departments to a liquidating firm. After a lapse of one year, our Mr. I. N. Babbitt made it possible for the resumption of the Glass Department by financing the purchase of the Glass and Silver Departments from the liquidating firm, but, only the Glass Department was operated, as it was very difficult to get metal for the Silver Department, at that time. This Glass Department was organized and incorporated under the title of the Gundersen Glass Works, Incorporated.

As you, no doubt, know, we manufacture the very highest type of Lead Potash crystal, cut, engraved, as well as plain glassware - strictly free-hand-made, no moulds being used whatsoever.

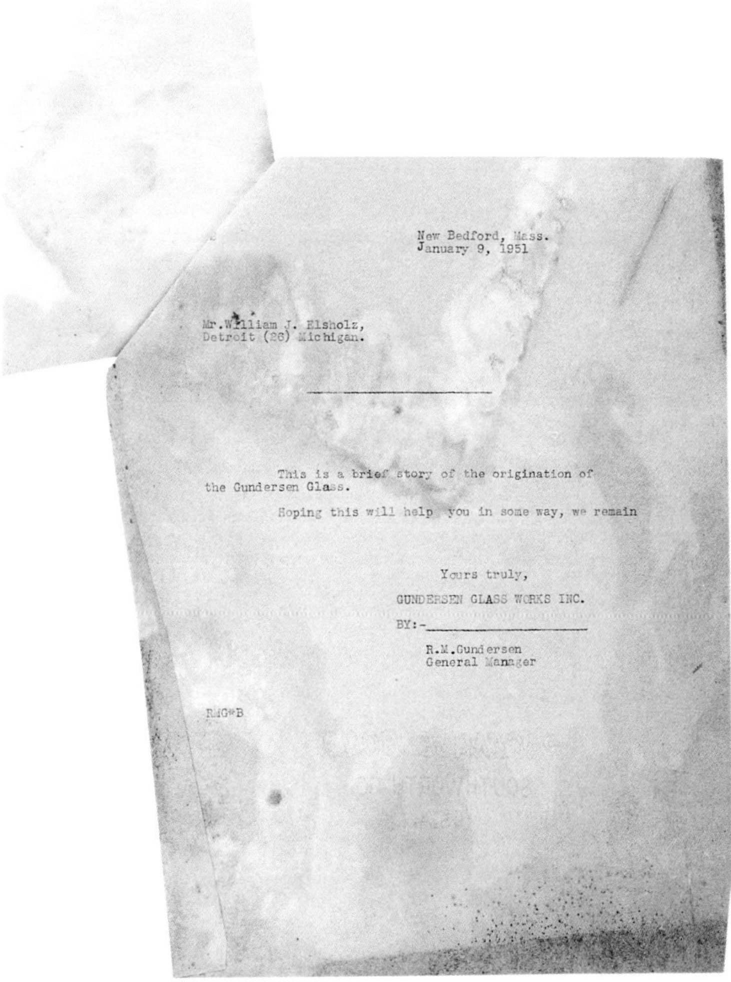

New Bedford, Mass.
January 9, 1951

Mr. William J. Elsholz,
Detroit (26) Michigan.

This is a brief story of the origination of the Gundersen Glass.

Hoping this will help you in some way, we remain

Yours truly,

GUNDERSEN GLASS WORKS INC.

BY:-

R.M. Gundersen
General Manager

RMG*B

Mt. Washington Glass

Famous names such as Deming Jarvis, William Libbey, Captain Henry Libbey, and Frederick Shirley appear throughout the nineteenth century as American glass companies opened and closed, were merged and sold. Their collective efforts, capital, and bold determination eventually resulted in the establishment of the Mt. Washington Glass Company in 1871, in New Bedford, Massachusetts. For the next couple of decades, under the guidance of Frederick Shirley, Mt. Washington became a major producer of fine Victorian art glass. Famous products known as Crown Milano, Royal Flemish, Burmese, Peach Blow, Napoli, Lava Glass, and others were developed and patented during this period. Popular in their day, these products are highly sought by the collector today. Mt. Washington Glass was also highly regarded and well-known for the beauty and quality of its brilliant-cut glass line which relied upon bold precision geometric cutting to enhance the beauty of the glass form.

An example of Mt. Washington's early Crown Milano glassware which, according to Leonard Padgett's book, *Pairpoint Glass*, was originally called Albertine. The trademark on the underside is the early version, believed to be the Albertine mark.

A Mt. Washington Lava Glass oil lamp which has the original patent label, #207077, dated August 13, 1878. The patent date, as well as patent number, indicates this item to actually be an example of Mt. Washington's "Rainbow" or "Iris" iridescent glass, which has an earlier patent date than the products specifically referred to as Lava Glass. We are not familiar enough, however, with Mt. Washington's products to differentiate between the two. We do know that items of this line are very rare.

A Mt. Washington White Lusterless Glass "pinch" vase decorated and signed by the "Smith Brothers".

A sampling of Mt. Washington's decorated White Lusterless Glass salt and pepper shakers.

A Napoli Glass tall comport by the Mt. Washington Glass Company. The gold tracing around the design has been applied to one side of the clear glass, while the actual design has been applied to the opposite side.

A beautiful Mt. Washington Mother of Pearl Satin Glass Bride's Bowl insert with gold decoration. The silver-plated Pairpoint frame, which would have contained the bowl, is missing.

Another great example of Mt. Washington's decorated White Lusterless Glass. This is one of a matched pair, and it is unclear whether it was decorated in-house or by the Smith Brothers.

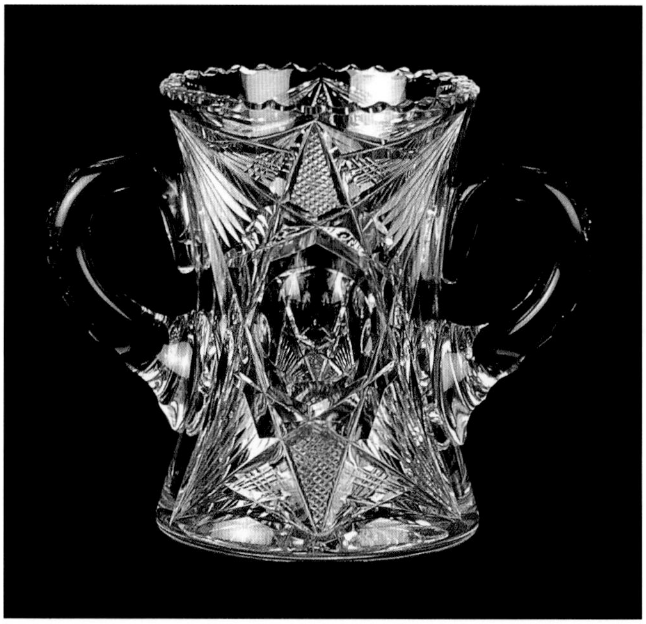

An example of Brilliant Cut Glass produced by the Mt. Washington Glass Company. The pattern on this spooner is known as "Malden".

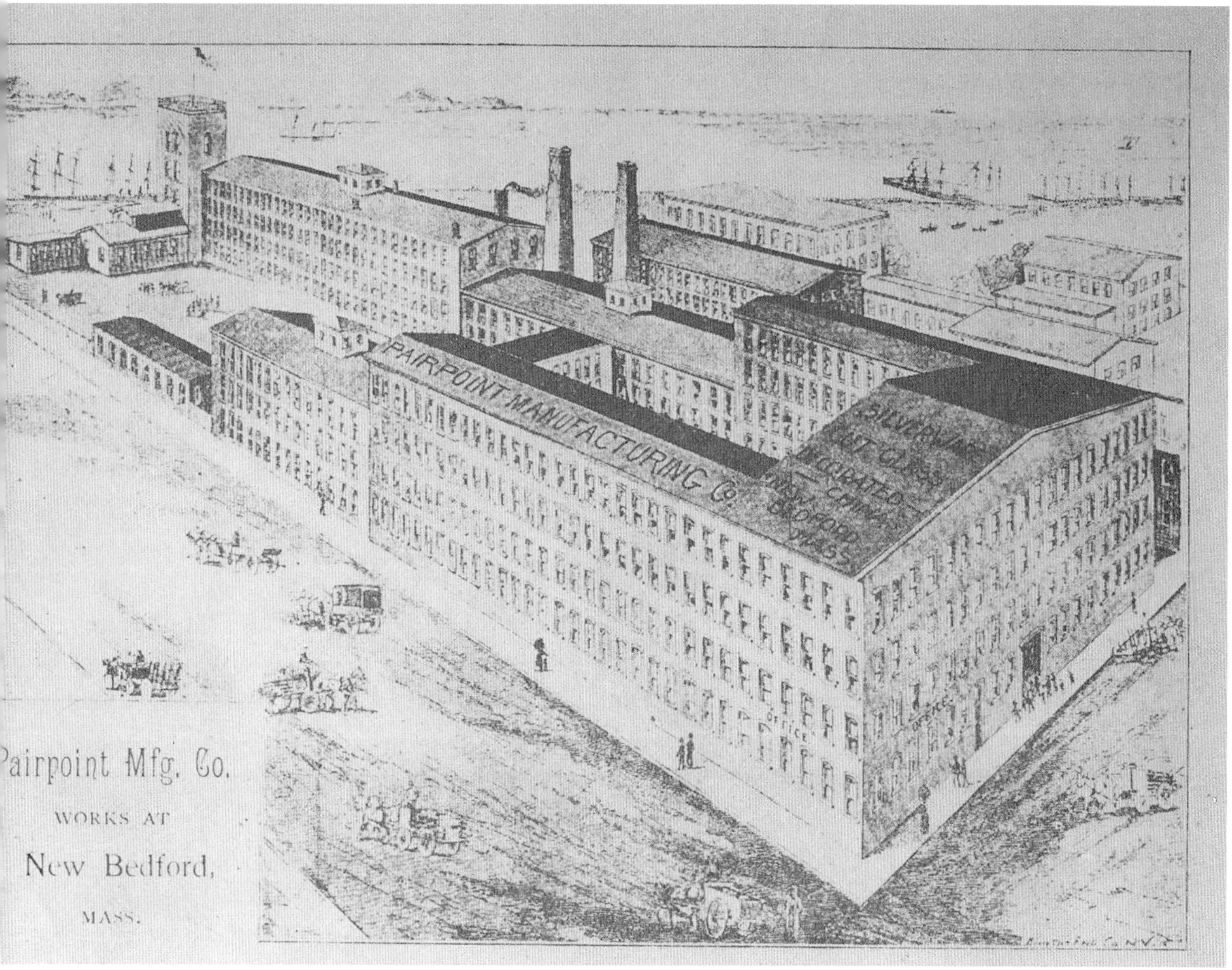

A view of the Pairpoint Manufacturing Co.'s factory buildings, in New Bedford, Massachusetts, as shown in the New Bedford Semi-Centennial Souvenir publication, date unknown. *Courtesy of Charles and Barbara Coulter.*

Silver Plated Fittings

One of the fashion trends of the day was to combine quality glass with fancy sterling silver or silver-plated metal fittings. Responding to this trend and to fulfill a growing public demand for silver-plated metal table and decorative items, Alexander H. Seabury, a principal of the Mt. Washington Glass Company, became one of the founding members, in 1880, of the Pairpoint Manufacturing Company. Named after the chief designer and short-tenured Thomas Pairpoint, a vast line of utilitarian and decorative silver-plated household items was offered to the public. By the early 1890s, Pairpoint had become one of the foremost makers of silver-plated goods in the United States, and no other company surpassed their quality.

A Pairpoint silver-plated jewel box, item #945, with the original gold satin lining. Originally this piece was factory-lacquered to retard tarnishing.

The impressed signature of the Pairpoint Manufacturing Company shown on the underside of the jewel box in the accompanying photograph. Pairpoint always included the item number in the immediate proximity of the trademark. The rectangular marking above and to the left of the trademark was where the original label, which stated the fact that the item had been lacquered, was attached. It came off during the silver replating process.

A Pairpoint brass and plated silver fern which has been professionally polished and relacquered.

The underside view of the brass and plated silver Pairpoint fern which shows the impressed signature of the Pairpoint Corporation, which succeeded the Pairpoint Manufacturing Company around 1900. The item number is directly below the trademark.

A Pairpoint silver-plated candlestick/chamberstick with a floral decorated White Lusterless Glass insert. This piece was originally factory-lacquered to retard tarnishing.

A signed Pairpoint decorated biscuit jar with silver-plated rim and lid. We believe this piece would have been called Crown Milano had it been marketed under the Mt. Washington Glass Co. name.

A detail view of the Pairpoint signature applied to the underside of the biscuit jar shown in the adjoining photograph.

Merger

The rapid growth of the Pairpoint Manufacturing Company resulted in on-going financial problems and business management stress. Since the Mt. Washington Glass Company had essentially the same ownership and customer base as the Pairpoint Manufacturing Company, the two companies were merged on July 14, 1894, and Pairpoint Manufacturing Company acquired the Mt. Washington Glass Company. For the next six years or so, the combined work force continued producing the product lines of each company respectively, merging product components, as they had done previously, according to the dictates of current styles and tastes. It was not uncommon to find similar products marketed under each company's name during this period. Occasionally you will find an item that combines metal and glass, such as the biscuit jar pictured, that has had a legitimate Pairpoint signature applied to the glass component. Previously the glass would have either had no signature or a signature identifying the Mt. Washington product line that it represented. By the late 1890s, the public's interest in the silver-plated metal wares and Victorian art glass products fell off.

The Pairpoint Corporation

The companies were reorganized once more in 1900, fully integrating the two companies and their product lines. Demand for fine brilliant-cut glass was strong, and Pairpoint was able to produce as much as the public could consume. As war in Europe expanded and the United States became involved, raw materials were diverted to wartime efforts. Men left their apprenticeships to serve their country; some never returned. Demand for fine luxuries diminished as attentions were diverted and changing tastes affected the popularity of brilliant-cut glass; its end was in sight.

A trend had been developing for several decades prior to World War I, for a different style of glass finishing. Notable in this regard was Mr. H.P. Sinclaire who had difficulty convincing his employer, Thomas G. Hawkes, to incorporate the new, lighter style of engraved decoration into the Hawkes product line, in spite of Sinclaire's engraving designs winning international awards at world-wide glass expositions. Frustration led H.P. Sinclaire to leave Hawkes, in 1901, to form his own company to produce his beautiful engraved glass for a market he believed was evolving. Other designers and glass producers also sensed the beginning of the public's changing interest away from heavy brilliant-cut glass products. As the new century got underway, designers' creativity flourished and the number of engravers working increased dramatically. The public clamored for products that incorporated these new engraving designs, most of which were based upon themes of nature. Ultimately, by 1918 and the end of World War I, the Brilliant Period of glass manufacturing ended.

1918

The major changes in glass decorating styles, by 1918, signal the start of this study of Pairpoint glass. Life in America changed dramatically then, as people gradually became more affluent and flamboyant in their lifestyles. Fashions became bold and highly stylized. The industrial revolution was creating volumes of affordable products. Immigrants with well-developed skills and strong work ethics followed their relatives to American shores to escape devastation in Europe and to make a new life. Many found their way to New Bedford, Massachusetts and the Pairpoint Corporation. The carriage trade demand was strong for high quality art and craft products, including crystal tablewares and accessories. Skilled glass workers and apprentices found work at Pairpoint.

New glass shapes and engraving designs abounded, color was introduced into glass, and the public went wild. Sales were strong, quality was unsurpassed anywhere in the world, foreign competition was only a minor annoyance, and the Stock Market was doing well...until 1929. The next decade was another story.

The 1930s saw dramatic change in American economics. As the Depression era set in, markets went flat and jobs were lost in every industry, including glass. The twenty year period from 1918 to 1938 are the Middle Years of the Pairpoint story, a time when their quality was particularly high and the variety of tablewares extensive.

An example of a Pairpoint Limoges dresser box. The porcelain blanks were imported from France and decorated by Pairpoint's decorating department.

A detail view of the Pairpoint Limoges signature applied to the dresser box in the adjoining photograph.

An example of H. P. Sinclaire's light engraving. This pattern is called "Atlanta" and has been applied to Sinclaire Candlestick #2948.

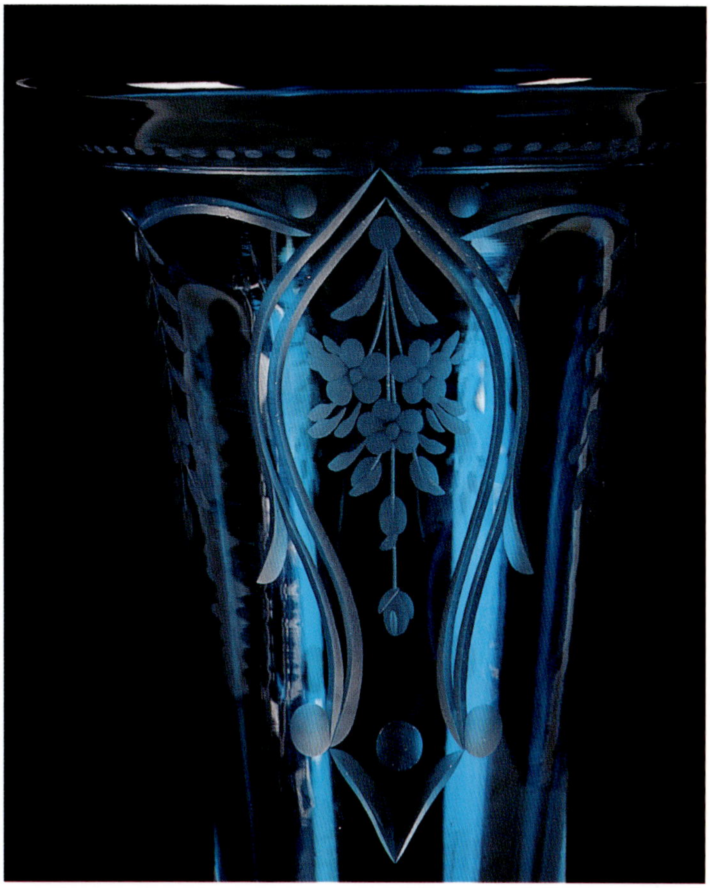

Another example of Sinclaire's light engraving style. This Colonia Blue Sinclaire Vase #13078, has been engraved in the "Vernon" pattern.

1938

The closure of the Pairpoint Corporation, in 1938, marks the end of the middle period of Pairpoint glass. As Europe, and then the United States, entered World War II, the manufacture of Pairpoint glass entered a new era. The Pairpoint operation was purchased by a group of local businessmen, which included master glassblower Robert Gundersen, in 1939. The revived Pairpoint operation continued in business as Gundersen Glass Works for another thirteen years, replicating the "old" product line upon demand while producing designs to satisfy new tastes in the rapidly changing market. Gundersen maintained high quality standards throughout his tenure, but the loss of experienced engravers through attrition, the unavailability of young men willing to endure the rigors of learning the glass trade, and the availability of cheaper goods on the market made it impossible to continue producing the caliber of goods available during the 1918 to 1938 period. The Gundersen period of glass manufacturing ended with the death of Robert Gundersen in 1952.

To study the chronological evolution of the Pairpoint Corporation and its management is certainly of value and interest to many, and is necessary to understanding their struggle for survival during the century of operations. But to limit one's perspective to the deeds, mortgages, bricks, steel, and mortar is to limit one's ability to contemplate and feel the essence of the glass tableware produced there. Rather, it is the evolution of the skilled craftsmen and artisans that remained constant throughout these years...the untethered creativity that gave purpose to the bricks and mortar. The quality of each glass item produced *at* Pairpoint, not *by* Pairpoint, was established and maintained by the craftsmen on a one-by-one basis, every hour, every day. How the gaffer or the engraver felt on any given day (whether his wife or son was ill, whether he longed for his parents who lived in England or Germany) caused his creativity to ebb and flow. Each piece was the expression of his natural and acquired skills and of his inner self, and he exposed himself to acceptance or rejection on a piece-by-piece, day-by-day basis. To hold and experience a piece of Pairpoint glass today is to see into the soul of its creator. For the collector to appreciate that craftsmen, long-since departed, had the inspiration and skill to create such works of art is to understand the beauty and to capture the *essence* of this glass.

THOMAS A. TRIPP
PRESIDENT

ISAAC N. BABBITT
TREASURER

GUNDERSEN GLASS WORKS INC.

SUCCESSOR TO THE PAIRPOINT CORPORATION

IN THE MANUFACTURE OF GLASS AND SILVER

-- TRADE (P) MARK --

NEW BEDFORD MASSACHUSETTS
U. S. A.

October 2, 1939.

ANNOUNCEMENT

Throughout the trade a legion of friends of "Pairpoint" quality glassware will welcome the announcement that production has been resumed at full capacity in all departments of the original factory under the name "Gundersen Glass Works, Incorporated".

The new corporation is successor to the Pairpoint Corporation in the manufacture of Glass and Silver, and will be directed by Mr. Thomas A. Tripp, President, Mr. Isaac N. Babbitt, Treasurer and General Manager, and Mr. Robert M. Gundersen, Works Manager.

Our President, Mr. Thomas A.Tripp, needs no introduction. His distinguished career in the glass industry was one of outstanding achievement. He will be remembered as the man who built and so successfully directed the destinies of the old company for more than half a century. In the history of American glass-making the name 'Thomas A. Tripp' is of national renown.

As Treasurer and General Manager, Mr. Isaac N. Babbitt will bring to the business the heritage of a long line of gifted New England mechanical geniuses, plus sound modern business methods of proven value as exemplified by his enviable personal record of successful business achievement.

To Works Manager, Mr. Robert M. Gundersen (from whom the new firm takes its name) goes credit for the supreme quality of Pairpoint Glass universally acknowledged as the standard of excellence. Supplementing his wizardry as a famous glass-maker, Mr. Gundersen is a master-craftsman of the highest order, a unique combination which places Gundersen Glass Works, Incorporated, in a pre-eminent position in the fine glass trade.

Under the direction of the well known designer, Mr. Floyd F. Cary and all the old staff of skilled glass workers and trained craftsmen, augmented by new thoughts, new methods and the new ideas demanded by consumers of today, the artistic level of the Pairpoint product will reach new heights, while still carrying on the honorable century old traditions of Pairpoint standards of quality and workmanship.

May we look forward to the continued pleasure of serving you.

Sincerely yours,
GUNDERSEN GLASS WORKS, INC.

An important letter, dated October 2, 1939, regarding the resumption of glassmaking activities by the Gundersen Glass Works, Inc. This letter was salvaged from the abandoned factory in the early 1960s by Charles Coulter along with a wealth of other internal documents and company correspondence. *Courtesy of Charles and Barbara Coulter.*

Chapter 2

Pairpoint Shapes and Blanks

A novice in the glass tableware field is wisely advised to "learn the shapes." Over time one intuitively realizes that shape recognition is the primary factor in recognizing Pairpoint glass (and other manufacturer's products as well). However, there also are many other factors to consider when determining attributions today. These factors are much more subtle than shape recognition alone, and are far more important when identifying or excluding a piece of glass as having been made by Pairpoint. The presence or absence of certain factors is sometimes critical and absolutely definitive when studying a shape that is generally similar between makers. Often the way an edge is finished, or the existence of an optic pattern, or resonance can provide exclusionary evidence that a piece was not made by the Pairpoint Corporation.

Two candlesticks that are very similar in their basic shapes. The one on the left is Pairpoint's #1600, shown engraved in the CORONAL pattern, and the one on the right is Sinclaire's #2948, engraved in their Atlanta pattern. Seen separately it would be easy to think they were from the same maker, but when viewed side by side, the design differences become readily apparent. Only time, experience, and practice will make it possible to recognize Pairpoint's shapes at a glance.

We have seen many examples of glass that are incorrectly attributed to Pairpoint; the incidence of misattribution could be as high as 35%. We don't believe, in most cases, that there is any intent to defraud the buyer. Instead the misattribution is the result of a lack of knowledge on the part of the seller. This is unfortunate because a seller's attribution presents itself as implied and authoritative knowledge and becomes *fact* to the buyer and becomes the basis that the buyer relies upon when making his own attributions in the future.

Certain *absolute* terms are used here, such as *never*, *always*, *every*, *will*, and probably others, to provide a strong sense of what you should expect to see, or not see, when examining a piece of Pairpoint glass. *Accept the use of these words with a certain degree of caution* as only an expert (or fool) in a field of study should ever take the risk of claiming strong beliefs as absolutes. Keep your mind open to new information that may appear unexpectedly. Just when you think you have it all figured-out, something or someone will come along to make you reassess your beliefs.

Size dimensions, when known, are given in nominal terms, such that an 8" comport may actually measure 7-7/8" or 7-3/4" or even 8-1/8" because every piece of Pairpoint glass was made by hand, and it is reasonable to expect some modest deviation in the actual dimensions.

It was common for Pairpoint to make several size versions of the same shape, however, we did not necessarily know all of the specific dimensions of all the size variants at the time we compiled our data. When this realization occurred we inserted an underlined blank space to signify that a piece of information is missing. That way there will be a space available for the reader to up-date his own copy in the event the information becomes known to him. Remember...this is a workbook; it's O.K. to write in it!

We nudge you forward into the world of Pairpoint shapes with enormous pleasure and great expectations. The information provided is the sum of all that we have learned, observed, and sensed during the last ten years of buying and studying Pairpoint products. We urge you to read this information carefully and refer to it often as you build your collection and your knowledge. Always remember that information can be both *inclusionary* as well as *exclusionary*, with the probability of the latter being more commonplace.

Uniformity of Size

Each example of Pairpoint glass was individually blown and shaped by a master craftsman. As a result of being made by hand, each piece will vary slightly in its final size. As a matter of fact, you should expect to find size variations as well as minor variations in shape when comparing two or more pieces of the same style blank. You may find the stem on one piece to be *fatter* than the stem of its mate. Foot diameters or thickness may also vary. These inconsistencies are proper and are definitive signs that a piece was individually formed by hand.

Thickness of Glass

You may recall an earlier reference to the uncertainty of destination at the time a blank was manufactured. It could have been intended to go immediately to the cutting/engraving department or into general inventory for sale as an undecorated blank, or held for future decorating to fulfill a special customer order. Although it was not always known how any specific blank would end-up, one thing was known for certain. Not all engraving patterns could be applied to *thin* blanks; the depth of cutting required to properly execute some designs would have gone through the glass and destroyed it. You will regularly find the same Pairpoint shapes made in varying thicknesses. If the piece you are examining is engraved, and it utilizes a thicker blank, the reason for the extra thickness will be obvious. It would not be common to find a lighter, more delicate design applied to a thick blank. When a shape is found unengraved (a plain blank), it most likely will be found with a thinner cross-section. This is probably due to two factors. If a blank was to be sold *plain*, the thinner variant presented better to the buyer (less *clunky*), and if a blank was to be decorated sometime in the future, most Pairpoint engraving patterns could be applied to the thinner cross-section blanks. You may occasionally come upon a plain blank that is *thick*, but it would probably be less appealing to the eye than the thinner variant.

Two Pairpoint #B-366 Comports positioned to show the variations in dimensions that you should expect to find when comparing similar items. This example also shows a variation in the intensity of the color, which also can be expected.

A comparison of two similar blanks made in different thicknesses to accommodate engraving/cutting patterns requiring different depths. The thinner one on the left has a shallow pattern, while the thicker one on the right has a deeper pattern.

A Depression glass creamer showing the mold seam line where indicated by the pointer. This line appears where the two halves of the mold were joined prior to molten glass being injected. *Courtesy of Clare Hintenach.*

Seam Lines, Mold Marks & Tool Marks

Pairpoint glass will never be found with seam lines or mold marks. We are sure you have all noticed ribs of glass or surface-dimpling and irregularities on mass-produced glass such as Depression Glass. This condition, which is usually more noticeable to the touch but very visible to the eye, is the result of forcing molten glass into a mold form that contains surface imperfections and joint seams that don't mate perfectly. Such items of glass are more a testament to the mold-maker's skill than to that of the glass blower. The sizing of mold-formed pieces will be uniform while the visible appearance could vary considerably due to the condition of the mold at any point in time. You will often see reference to earlier examples from a mold being sharper and better defined than later examples.

While most Pairpoint shapes were made individually by hand from a gather of molten glass, Pairpoint did use molds to create some shapes or optical effects within the glass itself. However, within their process, the use of a mold was simply an intermediate step of the manufacturing process, not the final step as with mass-produced glass products. After using a mold to define a shape, the glass would proceed to the hand finishing process where any evidence of mold lines would be eliminated. The nature of hand-working glass such as that done by the premier glass houses would result in the occasional presence of tool marks. This is perfectly acceptable so long as the toolmarks are not excessive and compromise the appearance and feel of the finished product. Every craftsman turned out his share of mistakes that were returned to the pot or sent to the cullet pile.

Some molded glass products were very well done and require very close examination. Some pieces were made by high-volume glass companies in an effort to simulate, or copy, popular styles produced by Pairpoint, and others. We have often seen these *look-alikes* represented as Pairpoint. If mold lines are present, they will be most noticeable in the area where a stem meets a bowl or foot. If there is any trace at all of a line or ridge, usually in two or three evenly spaced places around the circumference, then the item was NOT made by Pairpoint. In mass-produced mold-formed pieces, there will usually be other tell-tale signs that will help you make your determination. By utilizing the other information within this section, you won't be easily fooled.

The Bowl Bump

This is our name to describe the small bump or hump of glass at the bottom center of most hand-made comport and bowl-like forms. It is the thicker area of glass in the proximity of where a stem or foot is attached. (If no stem or foot is attached, there will not be a bowl bump present.) Since the glass is very plastic and semi-melted at the time a foot or stem is *stuck* to the bowl section, the pressure created by the attachment process causes the glass at the bottom of the bowl to bulge upward. This bump is present in probably 95% of all hand-blown glass and is never present (unless intentionally introduced) in most mold-formed glass. An exception could occur if a stem and bowl were mold-formed individually and joined later. While this bowl bump may not be helpful in

The Bowl Bump.

determining a Pairpoint provenance, its absence may well indicate a mold-formed origin, thus eliminating it from further consideration. Use this feature in conjunction with other known characteristics.

Edge Finishing

We use the term *edge* to describe that portion of any shape that is terminal in nature; the outer circumference of the opening of a bowl or vase, or the periphery of a foot or candle bobeche, or a transition shoulder or connecting wafer. Unless a blank is cut or engraved, and the pattern extends itself into edge decoration (which is obvious), Pairpoint ALMOST NEVER ground its edges in any way (see the *Grinding* section, which follows, for exceptions); all edges were left in their natural fire-polished state — smooth and rounded and a continuation of the flat surface. Except for an ever-so-slight thickening at the very edge, due to the pressure of the tooling work required to make a piece round, the edge will always be merely a smooth termination of the flat surface adjacent to it.

Pairpoint never folded their edges as is commonly found on many, but not all, of the products produced by Steuben and Sinclaire during this era. Pairpoint would occasionally apply a narrow band of contrasting color to the edge of their shapes to accommodate a specific design requirement such as the "cut-to-clear" technique used for the DARLINGTON pattern.

A folded edge as it appears on a Steuben Celeste Blue bowl. This type of edge finishing was very common on Sinclaire and Steuben products.

A fire-polished edge.

An example of a Pairpoint comport engraved in the DARLINGTON pattern. While manufacturing the blank, and before any engraving occurred, a thin band of the color Rosaria was applied to the portion that was to become the rim. During the engraving process, part of the pattern was *cut* through the Rosaria, allowing the clear glass to *show through*.

This is an example of one of the few Pairpoint glass products that will appear with a ground edge and no pontil mark. This is due to a variation in the way the object was held and rotated during manufacture. If you observe the bottom of the outer edge (the part that contacts the shelf) very closely, you can detect an ever-so-slight waviness in the reflected light. This is due to the hand grinding applied to smooth the rough glass edge during the final steps of manufacture. The light reflection also shows how smooth and well polished the edge is. Also note the absence of any pontil mark in the center of the recessed foot area.

Grinding

PLEASE USE CAUTION AND EXAMINE YOUR GLASS CAREFULLY! If you are relatively certain the piece of glass you are examining was made by Pairpoint, 99% of the time it WILL NOT have a ground edge. There are occasions where the technique of manufacture mandated that one of the normally fire polished edges would be finished by grinding; we have made a special effort to include this information within the caption, under the photograph or illustration, of each shape that is finished in this way. It is very possible that we have overlooked an example or two, or more, so we have a simple *test* you can use to determine whether edge grinding exists legitimately on any piece of Pairpoint glass you encounter. We have observed that Pairpoint objects with legitimately ground edges were not held and rotated directly on a punty rod during the final step of manufacture (see the upcoming paragraphs on *Pontil Marks*). Therefore, you will not find a pontil mark. If the item you are examining has both, then you are, with a high degree of certainty, dealing with a repaired item. When Pairpoint applied a ground finish to their edges, they did so with great skill. Their grinding is very flat with ever-so-slight chamfering on both the inside and outside corners. The ground surface was then polished to a high degree of smoothness and shine.

If you detect any edge grinding at all that does not seem to fit in with the exceptions described above, then you have a repaired or cosmetically enhanced piece. You would be amazed at the number of Pairpoint pieces we have seen over the years that have been repaired by grinding but not documented accordingly. Look carefully because some grinders are good, but we have never seen a glass grinder skilled enough to duplicate the fire-polished, slightly swelled edge as it came from the Pairpoint factory. (The closest to perfection that we have ever seen has been the work of Mr. Ed Poore, whose shop is located in Sagamore, Massachusetts, at 794 Sandwich Road. His only shortcoming is actually not his at all; the nature of grinding means that the newly formed edge will probably encroach upon any engraving design, if present.) To chronicle an example of the absurd, and to justify our advice about learning the shapes, we have to tell you of an experience we had several years ago. A glass dealer at a high quality glass show in Harrisburg, Pennsylvania tried to sell us a Pairpoint goblet. This *goblet* was actually a 12" Pairpoint urn-style vase (Shape #B-1083) that had been cut down to approximately 9" in height to eliminate severe damage. We have always wondered whether some inexperienced but joyful Pairpoint collector ever bought the piece and took it home, only to wonder once in a while why it looked a little *off*.

Quite regularly you will come upon a piece of glass made by Pairpoint or, more recently and commonly, by Gundersen that utilizes the famous *bubble ball* as its base. The grinding of the bottom, or underside, of the large bubble ball, for the purpose of finishing and leveling, is normal and is excluded from the comments of this section. However, this will be the only place on the specific piece that you should expect to find any signs of grinding.

BE WARY! Unless the Pairpoint item you are examining is extremely rare and desirable, stay away from repaired pieces. The market value is significantly reduced. On the other hand, if a repaired piece is comparatively inexpensive and suits your decorating needs, it may be a worthwhile purchase.

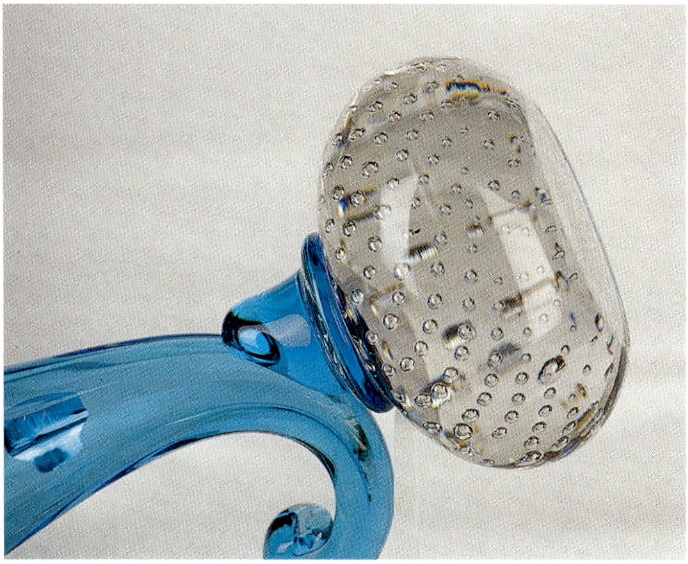

This is a partially inverted look at the bottom of a Marina Blue, Gundersen era cornucopia vase showing the flat-ground and polished area upon which the vase sits. Prior to finishing, which was necessary to level and stabilize the vase, this area was rounded and had a rough pontil mark.

Optics

An *optic* is the result of impressing a pattern or design into the basic form of a blank, while in its plastic, semi-molten state during production, to give a special optical effect when viewed. This technique has been widely used by many makers for many centuries. When utilizing the *optic* feature, the smooth, unbroken uniformity of the glass is transformed into a series of panels, swirls, or sections caused by a slight internal folding or crimping of the glass. Styles such as diamond optic, block optic, and panel optic as well as swirls and ribs are some of the many variations.

Pairpoint utilized the *optic* technique rather sparingly. This fact is extremely useful when examining those shapes that Pairpoint has in common with a few of the other high quality glass houses of the era. Except for a diamond optic pattern utilized only with the color Rosaria and a swirl optic pattern utilized within the special product line made for Carbone (see Special Products), Pairpoint almost never used optics as a decorative technique. For example we have a green compote that is virtually identical to Pairpoint's shape #A-228. Without the presence of a panel optic in the bowl portion, the ever-so-slight color variance may not have been enough to lead us to the conclusion that the compote probably was made by Fry. In this case the presence of a feature that should not have been there provided exclusionary evidence that the piece was not made by Pairpoint; the existence of the optic led us to study the color variance more closely.

An upward view of the bowl of a Rosaria Pairpoint comport showing a diamond optic pattern. Optic patterns were used very sparingly by Pairpoint, but are frequently found on objects made in this color. Many optic patterns were made by many glassmakers, but we have never seen any but the diamond optic pattern on Rosaria pieces.

A side-by-side comparison of two comports that could easily be attributed to the same maker, that being Pairpoint. The size variation, as well as the shape variation, could easily fall within the acceptable variations allowed hand-made items. The cobalt blue comport on the left is engraved in Pairpoint's Grape pattern, and is unquestionably a Pairpoint item. But, the green comport on the right utilizes a panel optic pattern within the bowl area, a feature you will not find on a Pairpoint comport of this shape. This feature, along with the notice of a slightly different hue of green, suggests that the green comport was made by the H.C. Fry Company. An identical green comport in our collection, which utilizes the bubble glass technique well-known to Fry, strengthens our attribution.

A detail view of what we believe to be Fry's Emerald Green comport showing the panel optic pattern formed within the glass.

An example of a rough pontil shown on the underside of the foot of an amethyst Bryden-Pairpoint Jack-in-the-Pulpit vase, probably made during the 1970s or 1980s. During our period of study, this pontil mark would have been ground and polished.

This rough pontil on an early Pairpoint candlestick is recessed approximately 1.5" into the dome-shaped foot and would not present any hazard to the surface of any piece of furniture upon which it may sit.

Pontil Marks & Finishing

The pontil mark is one of the easiest characteristics to recognize in determining whether a glass item was hand-worked. It is the mark that is left on a glass object after it has been *snapped-off* the steel punty rod which was used to hold and rotate the item during production. If left untouched the pontil mark will be rough and sometimes jagged, and it may display the pattern, if any, that existed on the end of the punty rod, such as a *waffle* impression. The absence of a pontil mark does not mean that an item was not hand-made, but its presence means that it probably was.

Although the existence of a pontil mark is a good sign that a piece of glass was hand-made, which it has to be if it came from Pairpoint, the method used to finish or remove the rough pontil mark is particularly useful when determining if the glass came from a quality maker. The pontil finishing method used can also aid in dating a Pairpoint piece to a general era of production. As you move about in your quest for quality glass decorative items, you will regularly hear terminology used to describe the various techniques used to finish the pontil marks. The understanding of this terminology is important.

ROUGH PONTIL - This is the condition whereby a pontil mark is left in its rough as-produced state with no attempt being made to smooth it at all. It is possible for the glass to be so rough that one could cut a finger if not careful. Generally a rough pontil is an indication that the glass item is of lesser quality, or from a non-U.S.A. maker, or is of a newer vintage, or a combination of all three. The finishing of a pontil mark was laborious and costly and could not be afforded on products being made to a lower price standard. And as far as current-day practices are concerned, the finishing of pontil marks seems to be of little concern and the lack of finishing does not seem to reflect negatively on the talent of the artisan or the perceived quality of his work.

At the risk of appearing contradictory, it is important to cite one exception to all that we have said about rough pontils being a sign of lower quality, price consciousness, or modern day origin. If Pairpoint or any of the other premier glass makers of the early twentieth century produced a design that incorporated a high-dome or bell-shaped foot, it was common practice to leave the deeply recessed pontil mark in its rough state. Since the rough pontil mark was relatively inaccessible and essentially *out of the way*, it would have been wasteful and inefficient to finish it.

GROUND PONTIL - This is a term that is widely used by glass people to describe the finishing technique applied to the rough pontil mark on hand-worked items of glass. It is a perfectly adequate term to describe what is effectively an intermediate level of pontil mark finishing. However, the use of the term inadvertently leads an inexperienced collector to draw an incorrect conclusion that the glass item in question must be of the highest quality due to the existence of a *ground pontil*.

Simply stated a ground pontil is just what it says. It is a rough pontil mark that has been removed by the application of a rounded grinding stone, leaving a concave depression where the punty rod had been attached. Ground pontils are generally smooth to the touch but retain a dull appearance. They are commonly found on Victorian-era glass, glass of foreign origin, and medium quality merchandise made in the United States. The shape of a ground pontil will often be somewhat oblong and irregular with no particular attempt being made to ensure the perfect roundness of the ground area.

NOTE...Do Not Presume that any assertion is being made that the existence of a *ground pontil* is an indication of medium quality. During the nineteenth and early twentieth century, it was the technique employed by most of the quality makers of fine art glass to smooth a rough

The dark age-stained ground pontil area stands in sharp contrast to the original shiny surface of this Victorian era, Smith Brothers-decorated White Lusterless glass vase, providing a wonderful illustrative example of *ground, but not polished*, pontil marks.

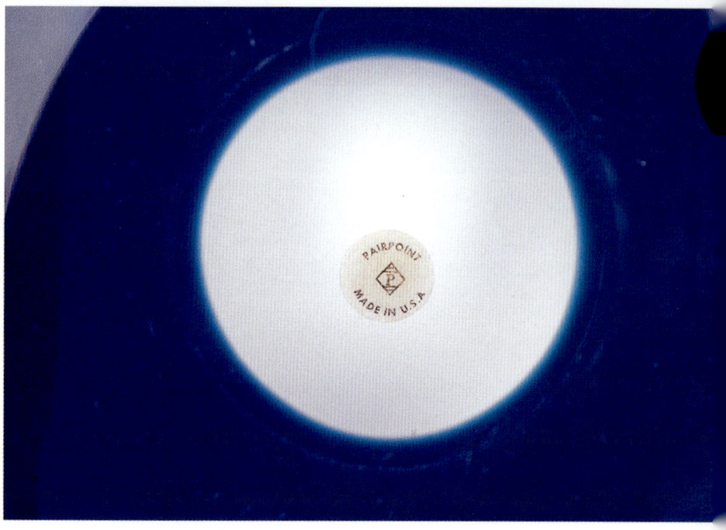

This photograph shows a completed polished pontil, on a cobalt blue cut-to-clear plate, through which can be clearly seen an old Pairpoint paper label measuring approximately 0.5" in diameter. This label is not attached. It is merely positioned to demonstrate the clarity of the polished glass.

We were fortunate enough several years ago to find this Pairpoint A-228 Comport that had never been completed. Not only does it illustrate the use of color overlay on its edge, but it shows the partially completed process of foot leveling and pontil mark grinding preliminary to the polishing procedure.

A detail view of the adjoining photograph showing the intermediate grinding of the pontil mark prior to polishing.

pontil, and was a sign of quality workmanship. The existence of a ground pontil is only an issue when attempting to attribute a glass item to Pairpoint or other quality maker during the period covered by this book.

POLISHED PONTIL - This is the term used to describe the process of polishing to a high brilliance the ground pontil described in the previous paragraphs. This process was used to convert the ugly blemish of the rough pontil mark into a virtual work of art. In addition to the high polish, the craftsman ensured that the finished pontil mark was round and concentric to the rest of the shape of the foot or bowl. So well done was the finish, sizing, and placement of the polished pontil that when observed from the normal position, the pontil mark was often undetectable by the eye.

The existence of a polished pontil on fine hand-worked glass made during the first three decades of the twentieth century should be expected. It is a hallmark of the quality of glass made during these years. The added expense could only be justified by the public's willingness to pay the higher price for quality goods.

Pairpoint Corporation was a premier manufacturer of fine glass products and, along with its contemporaries, utilized the polished pontil technique when finishing their glass. Except for those previously mentioned exceptions when a pontil was intentionally left rough or is absent due to the legitimate existence of a ground edge, every example of Pairpoint glass you will find will have a polished pontil. This includes stem ware, also. Upon occasion you will come upon a Pairpoint piece that is engraved and in-

An example of the engraver's skill applied to the rough pontil area on the underside of the foot of a Pairpoint #A-278 Comport in the MURILLO pattern.

corporates within its design an engraved flower or starburst under the foot that replaces the polished pontil. By touching the floral or starburst design, you will be able to feel that the area is recessed where the pontil mark would have been. The use of this technique to finish a rough pontil is particularly beautiful and demonstrates the skill of the engraver.

Unlike Steuben, which utilized an unusually small-diameter polished pontil on a regular, and predictable, basis, Pairpoint followed the convention of all the other fine glass makers of the day with regard to size. The pontil diameter will vary according to the size of the piece with the larger items having a larger diameter mark. Also, Pairpoint would enlarge a pontil mark if it would enhance an internal engraving design or improve the visual effect when looking into the bottom of a shape. The existence of a polished pontil is not particularly helpful when attributing glass items to Pairpoint. However, the absence of a polished pontil or engraved substitute is definitive exclusionary evidence.

A WORD OF CAUTION...Due to the great desire on the part of the early twentieth century public to possess examples of high quality glass such as that made by Pairpoint, and the inability of the masses to afford the real thing, many mass-producers of glass brought to market what might be known today as "knock-offs". Pieces that were very similar in shape and size were made available and provided the public the opportunity to own a decorative item that simulated what could only be afforded by the wealthy. We have seen glass items (a Fostoria low candlestick comes to mind) that have included a well-done molded-in fake pontil mark. If the collector would look closely for mold lines and other tell-tale characteristics, the "wannabe" pontil mark would ultimately be recognized for what it is. It's not that Fostoria or any other mass-producer of glass decorative items was attempting to defraud anyone, it was just their way of satisfying the market demand for fashionable look-alikes...like finding a dress "in the style of Versace" at K-Mart. If you utilize all the information available to you and avoid the tendency of most people to jump to conclusions, the problem of look-alikes will resolve itself in due course.

Grace of Design

This is an intangible and difficult, but important, concept to attempt to convey in words. It is like trying to describe beauty to another person; after all it resides in the eye of the beholder. But, that being said, if you were to look at the historical progression of style and design, you will see a cyclical repetition of certain characteristics that are pleasing to the human senses. It must be a genetic code within man that makes him appreciate and accept certain *things* over and over again even though fashions change. If you look at furniture styles, every one hundred years or so we have a *revival* of an earlier style which was a revival of an earlier style. The similarities that make a new fashion a revival of an old fashion can actually be boiled-down into basic design characteristics that are inherently pleasing to the eye...the curve of a cabriole leg or the proportion of a chest-on-chest.

Pairpoint glass products epitomize the best of the qualities that are inherently pleasing to the human eye, and in that context are merely copies of classic shapes and pro-

We know that we are on shaky ground when we start saying that one thing has more appeal than another, but we think the green Pairpoint #A-1062 Vase on the left exhibits more grace and balance of design than the red Fostoria Vase on the right. A distinctive characteristic of Pairpoint products is their use of full flowing curves and pleasing transitions.

portions. Curves that fully complete themselves and proportions that just feel right exist within Pairpoint's designs. Study your shapes and allow yourself to feel the *essence* of the glass. If you invest yourself in this way, you will be farther along in being able to identify Pairpoint glass than in any other way!

Bubble Ball

The bubble ball is a design element utilized by Pairpoint in many of their products made during the Middle Period and later into the Gundersen years. It is probably the most identifiable characteristic of Pairpoint products, but also the source of most mis-identification. The bubble ball is a sphere of clear glass that has been formed into a mold containing an array of spikes or projections. These spikes cause to be introduced a tiny trap of air within the glass sphere. Upon the removal of the glass sphere from the mold, the spike penetrations flow closed leaving a pattern of bubbles inside the *bubble ball*. After an additional coating of molten glass, the bubble ball is then attached to other components to form a complete design such as a bowl or a comport or some other item.

A detail view of Pairpoint's famous *bubble ball* showing the uniformity of bubble size and their upward spiraling pattern.

A full view showing how the bubble ball feature is incorporated in the overall design. The size of the bubble ball will vary with the size of the item, but will always retain a *proper* and balanced proportion. As the size of the bubble ball increases or decreases, the size of the bubbles within the ball will change proportionally. This example shows Pairpoint's #B-1485 Vase, with a square foot, in Rosaria cut-to-clear, cut in the LINCOLN pattern.

An example of an amethyst vase made by Erickson showing a very large bubble ball base. Just one of the several users of the bubble ball feature, Erickson's bubble ball bases are larger, higher, and have proportionally smaller bubbles than those of Pairpoint. Often attributed to Pairpoint, Erickson products are noticeably different in all ways than those of Pairpoint. Once you have seen several examples of Erickson's products, it would be hard to confuse the two.

An example of Pairpoint's #B-1627 Candlestick in Amethyst with an Amethyst bubble ball connector. To find a Pairpoint item with a colored bubble ball is the adult equivalent of getting your first bicycle from Santa Claus.

A detail view of the amethyst bubble ball connector showing the detail arrangement of the bubbles.

There has been a great lack of information available to the general public about Pairpoint glass; Pairpoint glass has been hard to identify for years. It should not be a surprise then to anyone that there exists a very high rate of mis-identification in the marketplace. The one known identifying characteristic, which is the bubble ball, provides the basis for attributing anything with a bubble ball to Pairpoint, and therein lies the root of mis-attribution. Many companies utilized the bubble ball within their product lines, but none used it as much as Pairpoint did. Fortunately the use of the bubble ball by other glass makers was in a way, or within designs, that are easily differentiated from Pairpoint designs, once you have the knowledge. There are usually enough other exclusionary characteristics, such as shapes or colors, that make it fairly easy to reject an item from being considered as Pairpoint.

If you look closely at Pairpoint's bubble ball, you will find a very uniform, evenly spaced, pattern of bubbles that appear to move upward in a spiraling manner. This is not unique to Pairpoint, but is always existent with Pairpoint. The bubble patterns in other makers' bubble balls may be irregular with great variations in the relative size of the bubbles within a single bubble ball. Other makers, such as Union Glass Company, have uniformity in their bubble size, but the pattern of the bubbles is vertical instead of spiraling, as with Pairpoint. And there are yet other makers whose attempt at making a bubble ball is so crude and poor that they self-disqualify in the attribution contest.

When viewing Pairpoint bubble balls, which are made in different sizes depending upon the overall design of the item, look for a uniformity in bubble size and a vertical spiraling. It is perfectly normal to find the occasional errant bubble or somewhat erratic spiral. After all, every artisan has a bad day now and then!

BE CAUTIOUS of anyone representing a piece of glass as Pairpoint solely on the strength of the presence of a bubble ball. And watch out for Union Glass pieces being represented as Pairpoint. Union's glass is very nice and had many design similarities when compared to Pairpoint. Although Union's colors are distinctively different from Pairpoint's colors, a fact which seems to go unrecognized, the big difference is in the bubble ball. The Union Glass bubble ball, which is very, very similar to Pairpoint's has its bubbles arranged in a vertical format without any spiral effect. Of the ten or twelve pieces of Union Glass we have seen over the years, all but one had been attributed to Pairpoint.

There are two variations of the bubble ball that are extremely scarce and worthy of mention. If you are fortunate enough, you may come upon either or both of the variants during your travels; if you do, and the items are available for purchase, we would strongly suggest that you do so.

Colored Bubble Ball - 99.95% of all the Pairpoint bubble balls you will see will have been made from clear/colorless glass, regardless of the color of the remainder of the item. However, Pairpoint did occasionally make the bubble ball from the same color as the rest of the item. To be perfectly correct, we believe the clear bubble ball was actually cased or overlaid with the colored glass, lest the shade of color would be so dark, due to the thickness of the ball, as to render the small bubbles practically invisible. The *only* example of this variant we have ever seen is in our collection; we purchased an amethyst candlestick in 1998, from Charles and Barbara Coulter, dealer friends of ours from So. Easton, Massachusetts.

Hollow Bubble Ball - Actually not a "bubble" ball at all, but serving the identical design function, this variant has no bubbles within the sphere of glass. Instead it is obviously *hollow* and is made from the same color of glass as the rest of the piece. We have seen only four examples of the Hollow Ball connector in over ten years. One was an amethyst vase for sale in Adamstown, Pennsylvania seven or eight years ago that was well above our financial means, the second was a clear engraved vase photographed on Page 90/Bottom of Leonard Padgett's book *Pairpoint Glass*, the third example is a red console set in our collection made during the later Gundersen era, and the fourth is an amber vase that we purchased recently for our collection.

EXPECT THE UNEXPECTED. This is a perfect time to remind the reader that Pairpoint did many unusual things within their product lines. The two bubble ball variations just mentioned are superb examples to support our earlier comments about not allowing yourself to believe that you know everything there is to know about Pairpoint glass. Until we saw and purchased the first example containing a colored bubble ball, our prior experience would have allowed us to conclude that such a thing did not exist. Keep your eyes and mind open!

An example of Pairpoint's #B-1083 Vase in Auroria with an Auroria hollow ball connector. Pairpoint items with hollow ball connectors are very scarce; to find one would be like getting your first bicycle, complete with Roy Rogers saddle bags, from Santa Claus.

A detail view of the Auroria hollow ball connector.

Use of Prisms

It was very fashionable through most of Pairpoint's Middle Period to incorporate glass prisms within designs. They appeared everywhere...chandeliers, tabletop lighting, and decorative accessories. Pairpoint was no stranger to the use of prisms in their designs, and they used all three of the most common types which we call the spear, the blunt, and the faceted drop prism. Except for several designs which specifically included prisms and are shown with prisms in this section, most Pairpoint shapes will be found unadorned. Do not be surprised, however, if you find a normally plain Pairpoint shape sporting a fine set of prisms. Although not common, prisms could be added to any shape whose design could lend itself to their inclusion. We have seen bowls, comports, and candlesticks that have been adapted to the use of prisms. Unless you are one that hates prisms, expect to pay more if the piece you are contemplating includes them.

This Pairpoint #B-1811 Candlestick in Green is typical of the many designs that utilized glass prisms. Their use in most cases was optional, but there are some designs that will always be found with prisms.

The "Spear" prism (left), the "Blunt" prism (center), and the "Faceted Drop" prism (right).

BE CAUTIOUS when thinking of paying a premium price for a piece of Pairpoint having prisms. Most pieces we have seen have lost their original prisms and someone has replaced them with an incorrect substitute. If authenticity and accuracy is important to you, and it should be, then spend some time studying the way Pairpoint used prisms. We have made every attempt to provide accurate dimensional and style information on those designs that incorporated prisms. Pairpoint predominately used spear and blunt prisms which can be expensive and hard to find today. Most substitutions will be the very common faceted drop prisms because they are the easiest to find. If you are going to pay that premium price for a prism-equipped item, be sure to allow for the cost of replacement prisms to make your acquisition authentic. A price of $5.00 each for a spear or blunt prism at a flea market would not be unusual. If you come across blunt prisms, you should pick them up on speculation...they are much harder to find than the spear prisms.

As you read the label "CLEAR/COLORLESS", keep in mind that you are reading THROUGH 2.50" of glass, the width of the square foot on a Pairpoint #5000 Goblet.

CLARITY OF GLASS: The formulation and mixing of Pairpoint's glass batch recipes was a critically precise operation. The quality and consistency of their raw component ingredients and the accuracy of their preparation resulted in a finished glass product that is absolutely clean and clear when held to a light source. Looking through Pairpoint glass at an object in the room is virtually the same as looking through optical quality glass; the object can be seen clearly with minimal distortion. So clear is Pairpoint's glass, that when one looks through the full 2-1/2" width of the thick glass foot on a water goblet we own, an object on the other side can be clearly seen with virtually no distortion or blurring.

SOUND: So far throughout this book we have regularly used sensual terms to describe the experience of studying Pairpoint glass products. We have asked you to *sense* the glass, *feel the essence* of the glass, and to get a *feel* for the glass. We have appealed to your visual sense when studying shapes or seeing colors or appreciating the clarity of the medium. And we have appealed to your sense of touch when describing the quality of finish and fabrication. Now we want to appeal to your sense of hearing as part of the understanding of Pairpoint glass.

We know intellectually and understand the physics of why it could be dangerous to *ring* our glass, and we are warning you against such a practice, but you have never heard a more beautiful sound than that of a ringing Pairpoint bowl. Now, we don't mean to suggest that you hit the glass with a mallet, or your shoe, but a gentle flick of your finger will really reward your senses. Naturally, different shapes, thicknesses, and colors will sound and resonate differently, but the sound of Pairpoint glass in any case is distinctive.

The sound of the glass is actually a very important diagnostic factor when determining attribution. The glass made by different companies will *ring* very differently, and the difference is very apparent. Whereas Pairpoint glass generally rings more like a church bell (there are variations from color to color), Sinclaire and Steuben glass items ring with a flat tone. Experiment at every opportunity, and when you become familiar with the respective sounds made by objects produced by other makers of glass, you will discover that sound becomes a very valuable exclusion tool when considering attribution.

A WORD TO THE WISE...Don't ever enter the display booth of a glass dealer and start ringing the dealer's glass. To some dealers this is tantamount to saying that their child is ugly and their grandmother wore combat boots. If you are seriously interested in a piece for sale, and ringing the glass gently is important to you, ask for permission.

Signatures

Pairpoint glass during the Middle Period was never signed. Period! Paper labels were applied, but they came off easily over the years as the glass was washed. It would be very unusual to find a piece of Pairpoint glass with the original label. We have never had occasion over the years to suspect that anyone was counterfeiting the old labels, but recently we are developing a suspicion that it could be happening. If you follow the process we have set forth in this book, the existence of a label should be little more than icing on the cake.

A HUMBLING CONTRADICTION: As you have undoubtedly come to realize by now, we believe strongly in the importance of remaining open-minded as you pursue your study of Pairpoint glass. And, there is no better example of

An original Pairpoint paper label.

the legitimacy of this belief than the recent discovery of information that contradicts the universal "fact" that Pairpoint never permanently signed their work. Approximately one month after we submitted our manuscript to the publisher, we started the arduous task of going through the thousands of original factory documents in our possession. Among these documents are many customer purchase orders and the resulting factory invoices dating from the late 1940s to the early 1950s, a time frame ten to fifteen years beyond our primary period of study. It is well known and documented that during these later Gundersen (1939-1952) and Gundersen-Pairpoint (1952-1957) production years, orders to replicate the earlier Pairpoint designs were regularly accepted and fulfilled. We have several examples of factory documents specifying, upon customers' request, that items be signed "Pairpoint" or "G-P" using a diamond drill. Although Pairpoint did not typically permanently sign their work, they could have, and the successor companies to Pairpoint certainly DID sign their work when requested to do so.

During the Middle Period, Pairpoint produced their *Fine Arts Line* (discussed later in the Special Products chapter) which was a new name for the old-style Pairpoint Manufacturing Company products that combined silver-plated metal components with clear or colored glass that had been engraved or cut. The metal portions of these items will always be stamped with Pairpoint's name as well as an item number.

AND THAT'S IT! If a piece of Pairpoint glass has a signature, and it is not specially marked as described above, then it is either faked or the glass item is a modern day product, currently being hand-made by Pairpoint Crystal, on Route 6-A in Sagamore, Massachusetts, a revival successor of the original Pairpoint Corporation.

BE CAUTIOUS when relying on the existence of a signature to establish the attribution of a glass item to any particular maker. Signatures can be faked, and frequently are, while the other characteristics cannot be!

An example of the stamped signature typically found on Pairpoint's Fine Arts Line products.

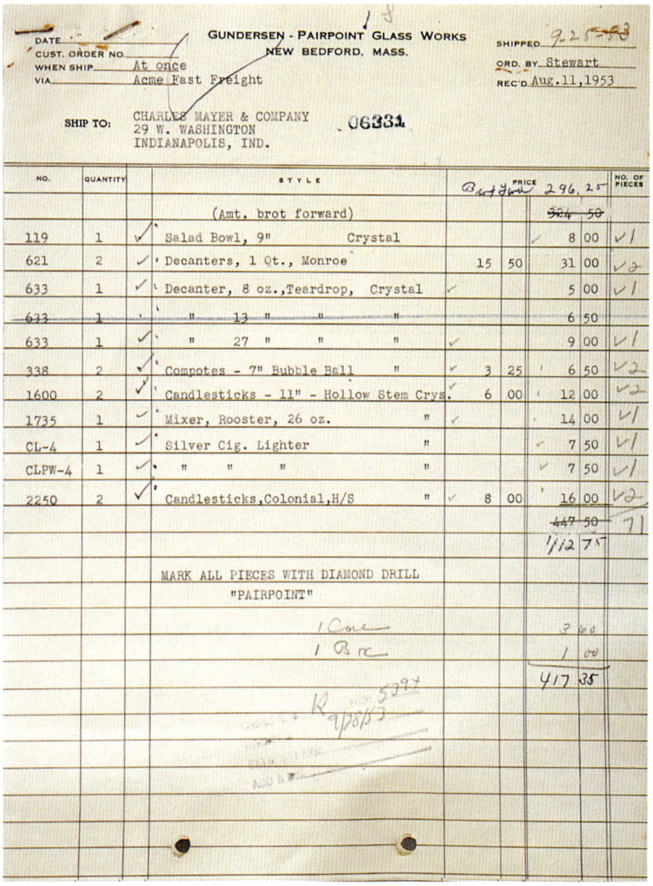

GUNDERSEN - PAIRPOINT GLASS WORKS
NEW BEDFORD, MASS.

DATE
CUST. ORDER NO.
WHEN SHIP At once
VIA Acme Fast Freight

SHIPPED 9-25-53
ORD. BY Stewart
REC'D. Aug.11,1953

SHIP TO: CHARLES MAYER & COMPANY
29 W. WASHINGTON
INDIANAPOLIS, IND.
06331

NO.	QUANTITY	STYLE	PRICE		NO. OF PIECES
		(Amt. brot forward)		~~324 50~~	
119	1	Salad Bowl, 9" Crystal		8 00	1
621	2	Decanters, 1 Qt., Monroe	15 50	31 00	2
633	1	Decanter, 8 oz.,Teardrop, Crystal		5 00	1
~~633~~	~~1~~	~~" 13 " " "~~		~~6 50~~	
633	1	" 27 " " "		9 00	1
338	2	Compotes - 7" Bubble Ball "	3 25	6 50	2
1600	2	Candlesticks - 11" - Hollow Stem Crys.	6 00	12 00	2
1735	1	Mixer, Rooster, 26 oz. "		14 00	1
CL-4	1	Silver Cig. Lighter "		7 50	1
CLPW-4	1	" " " "		7 50	1
2250	2	Candlesticks,Colonial,H/S "	8 00	16 00	2
				~~447 50~~	
		MARK ALL PIECES WITH DIAMOND DRILL "PAIRPOINT"			

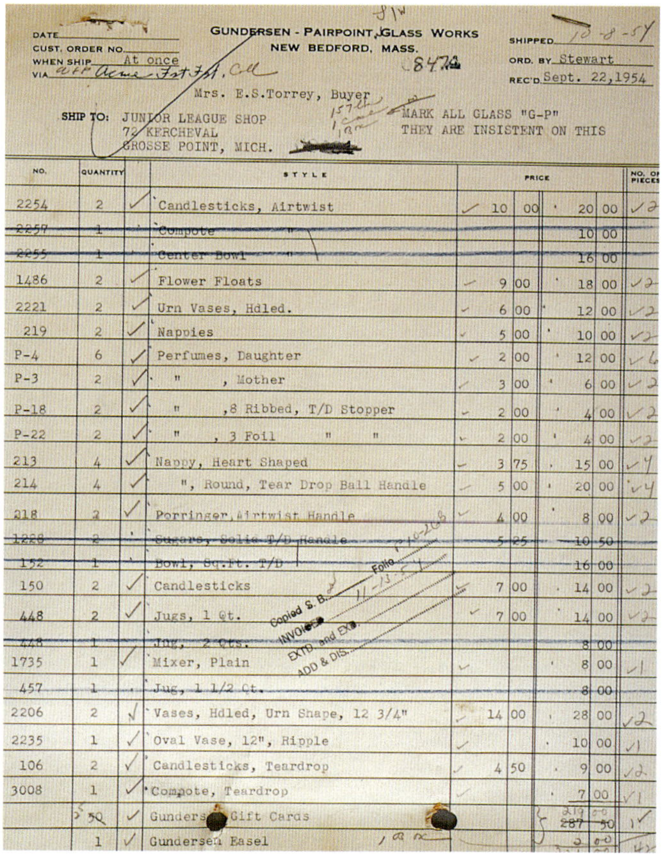

GUNDERSEN - PAIRPOINT GLASS WORKS
NEW BEDFORD, MASS.

DATE
CUST. ORDER NO.
WHEN SHIP At once
VIA

SHIPPED 10-8-54
ORD. BY Stewart
REC'D. Sept. 22,1954

Mrs. E.S.Torrey, Buyer

SHIP TO: JUNIOR LEAGUE SHOP
72 KERCHEVAL
GROSSE POINT, MICH.

MARK ALL GLASS "G-P"
THEY ARE INSISTENT ON THIS

NO.	QUANTITY	STYLE	PRICE		NO. OF PIECES
2254	2	Candlesticks, Airtwist	10 00	20 00	2
~~2257~~	~~1~~	~~Compote "~~		~~10 00~~	
~~2255~~	~~1~~	~~Center Bowl "~~		~~16 00~~	
1486	2	Flower Floats	9 00	18 00	2
2221	2	Urn Vases, Hdled.	6 00	12 00	2
219	2	Nappies	5 00	10 00	2
P-4	6	Perfumes, Daughter	2 00	12 00	6
P-3	2	" , Mother	3 00	6 00	2
P-18	2	" ,8 Ribbed, T/D Stopper	2 00	4 00	2
P-22	2	" , 3 Foil " "	2 00	4 00	2
213	4	Nappy, Heart Shaped	3 75	15 00	4
214	4	", Round, Tear Drop Ball Handle	5 00	20 00	4
218	2	Porringer,Airtwist Handle	4 00	8 00	2
~~1228~~	~~2~~	~~Sugars, Solid T/D Handle~~	~~5 25~~	~~10 50~~	
~~152~~	~~1~~	~~Bowl, Sq.Ft. T/D~~		~~16 00~~	
150	2	Candlesticks	7 00	14 00	2
448	2	Jugs, 1 Qt.	7 00	14 00	2
~~448~~	~~1~~	~~Jug, 2 Qts.~~		~~8 00~~	
1735	1	Mixer, Plain		8 00	1
~~457~~	~~1~~	~~Jug, 1 1/2 Qt.~~		~~8 00~~	
2206	2	Vases, Hdled, Urn Shape, 12 3/4"	14 00	28 00	2
2235	1	Oval Vase, 12", Ripple		10 00	1
106	2	Candlesticks, Teardrop	4 50	9 00	2
3008	1	Compote, Teardrop		7 00	1
	50	Gundersen Gift Cards			
	1	Gundersen Easel			

Copied S. B.
INVOICED
EXTD and EXD
ADD & DIS.
Folio

Two examples of original factory invoices, dating from the Gundersen-Pairpoint era (1952-1957), which specifically instruct that all glass items are to be signed either "G-P" or "Pairpoint". We have numerous factory invoices with the same stipulation. *Courtesy of Charles and Barbara Coulter.*

Important Pricing Guidelines

When you view each of the shapes that are shown in this chapter and take notice of the price range associated with each shape, you must remember that *the pricing is for the generic shape only, not the specific photographic example or illustration shown*. Pairpoint offered to make every shape in their general line in any color and with or without any decorating pattern. Depending upon which combination was selected by the consumer many years ago, the current retail value will fall somewhere within the price range shown. To determine the approximate value of your specific item, we refer you to the end of the *Values and Desirability* section where a valuation worksheet is provided for your convenience.

As you review the following pages, you will notice that Pairpoint made many of their shapes in various sizes with proportional perfection. When you see the pricing range for any given shape, and that shape has a variety of sizes, the pricing will refer to the size that has been enclosed within parentheses (...). You can reasonably expect to find that pricing will fluctuate up or down with the size variants; there is no general rule of thumb as to how much of a price difference there will be. This depends solely on the specific shape in question, and how popular and desirable that shape happens to be. The larger size of a popular shape with all the "right" characteristics will usually command a considerably higher price than its junior-sized counterpart. Also, the addition of a lid or cover to an item not shown being available that way will increase the normal value of that piece by a reasonable margin.

If you are a veteran collector and have had the occasion to study Pairpoint catalog plates from the late Brilliant period, you may notice a numbering system conflict. It would seem that when Pairpoint discontinued the manufacture of some of the earlier shapes, they made those shape identification numbers available for reuse at a later date. We are using the identification numbers that our research has determined were assigned to the represented shapes during the later Middle Period under study.

And finally, as you look at all of the photographs and illustrations that follow, remember that there are more shapes and variations than what we have shown; we just haven't discovered them yet. Keep your mind open and your senses tuned; maybe you will find them!

Bowls

The price ranges shown in the captions for each photograph or illustration refer only to the specific shape shown, without decoration. If the item shown includes some form of decoration, it is just happenstance, and should not be considered as a contributing element to the price range.

BOWL #A-106, Ruby Red, 13" d x 2.5" h. (Available with a wire mesh flower screen insert which will increase the price to some degree.) $150-400.

BOWL #A-109, cut in the MANSFIELD design, 8.50" d, (13" d). Pairpoint referred to the 8.50" d size as a comport. *Illustration from a Pairpoint Catalog*. $300-600.

BOWL #111, Clear, engraved in the COLIAS pattern, (8" d x 3.25" h), 9" d x __" h, 10" d x __" h. $100-375.

FLOWER BOWL #A-142, engraved in the CORONAL pattern with festooning. *Illustration from a Pairpoint Catalog*. $200-450.

FOOTED BOWL #A-145, Green, engraved in the GRAPES pattern, 10.50" d x 5.25" h, (12.50" d x 5.25" h), 14.50" d x 6.25" h. $200-500.

CENTERPIECE BOWL on PLATE #A-192 (one-piece), engraved in the HAMPTON pattern. *Illustration from a Pairpoint Catalog*. $250-550.

BOWL/NAPPY #210, 7" d.
BOWL/NAPPY #210.5, (8" d), 9" d, 10" d. *Illustration from a Pairpoint Catalog*. $100-375.

BOWL #A-193, engraved in the HAMPTON pattern. *Illustration from a Pairpoint Catalog*. $250-500.

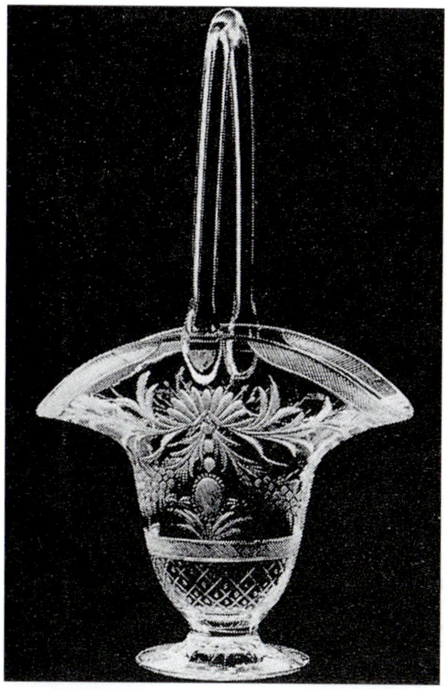

BASKET #A-237.5, engraved in the BUCKINGHAM pattern, __" h, (__" h), __" h. *Illustration from a Pairpoint Catalog*. $300-600.

BOWL #A-194, Rosaria with diamond optic, 8" d x __" h, 9" d x 3" h, 10" d x __" h, (12" d x 3.75" h), 14" d x 4" h, 16" d x __" h. $175-600.

BOWL #304, engraved in the GRAPES pattern, 9" d. *Illustration from a Pairpoint Catalog*. $125-375.

LILY DISH #348, cut/engraved in the VISCARIA pattern. *Illustration from a Pairpoint Catalog*. $175-550.

BOWL #313, engraved in the ENGLISH pattern. *Illustration from a Pairpoint Catalog*. $250-550.

BOWL #323, cut in the Brilliant-era design Caldonia (not shown in the Decorating Patterns chapter), (9.50" d), 10.5" d. *Illustration from a Pairpoint Catalog*. $200-575.

BOWL #B-368, engraved in the DEW DROP DESIGN, No. 218. *Illustration from a Pairpoint Catalog*. $200-500.

BOWL #B-369, Clear, engraved in the MAYFAIR pattern, 10" d x 6" h, (12" d x 6.75" h). *Gift from Georgiana Frost Saulsbury*. $200-550.

FISH BOWL #B-371, engraved in the DEW DROP DESIGN, No. 218, 10.50" d x 12" h. *Illustration from a Pairpoint Catalog*. $350-700.

BOWL #1010, cut/engraved in the VISCARIA pattern, (10" d x 3.50" h), 12" d x 4"h. (Available with a wire mesh flower screen insert which will increase the price to some degree.) *Illustration from a Pairpoint Catalog*. $250-550.

BOWL #A-1065, Canaria, engraved in the GRAPE pattern, 10" d x 4.50" h, (12" d x 5.25" h). $250-600.

BOWL # B-1065, Amethyst, 12" d x 6.75" h. $300-650.

FLOWER HOLDER #A-1091, engraved in the COLIAS pattern. *Illustration from a Pairpoint Catalog*. $200-575.

Right:
BOWL #A-1106, engraved in the ROCKFORD pattern. *Illustration from a Pairpoint Catalog*. $250-550.

BOWL #1174, Auroria, 5.75" d x 5.50" h. (Available with a wire mesh flower screen insert which will increase the price to some degree.) $125-300.

FLOWER GLOBE # Unknown 01, engraved in the GARLAND pattern, Small, (Medium), Large. *Illustration from a Pairpoint Catalog*. $175-475.

BOWL # Unknown 02, Auroria, (13" d), 15" d. (Sometimes referred to as the "Merry Widow" bowl according to George C. Avila's book, *The Pairpoint Glass Story,* Page 117.) $225-600.

BOWL # Unknown 03, Clear, cut/engraved in the GLENMORE pattern, (14" d x 3.25" h), 16.5" d x 3.50" h. $250-650.

Left:
BOWL # Unknown 05, Canaria, 10.50" d x 6.75" h, (12" d x 6.75" h). $250-550.

BOWL # Unknown 06, Cobalt Blue, 13" d x 4" h. Although we have never seen this shape other than as shown, it is extremely likely that it would have originally been part of the Fine Arts Line and would have been fitted to a silver plated metal base framework. $150-400.

BOWL # Unknown 07, Clear, engraved in the BUCKINGHAM pattern, 11.50" d x 7.50" h. It should be noted that, while this shape will be found as shown, it was originally intended to sit into a silver plated metal framework and would have been part of the Fine Arts Line of decorative products. When found as originally intended, the total height would have been 8.75". $175-500.

BOWL # Unknown 08, Clear, engraved in the MURILLO pattern, 9" d x 2.75" h. $150-550.

Candlesticks

The price ranges shown in the captions for each photograph or illustration refer only to the specific shape shown, without decoration. If the item shown includes some form of decoration, it is just happenstance, and should not be considered as a contributing element to the price range.

When pricing candlesticks it is important to remember that a pair will generally command a premium price over that of a single candlestick. In other words, one candlestick will generally sell for less than one-half of the price for a pair. The price ranges we show in this section are for a single candlestick.

CANDLESTICK #642, cut/engraved in the MURILLO pattern, 9" h with (10) 5" blunt prisms. (The prisms were intended as part of the shape design.) *Illustration from a Pairpoint Catalog*. $250-550.

CANDLESTICK #1600, Green, engraved in the BELVEDERE pattern, 8" h, 9" h, (10.75" h), 12" h, 14" h, 16" h. $175-400.

CANDLESTICK #1616, Clear, engraved in the HAMPTON pattern, 10.5" h with (8) 3" spear prisms. (The prisms were intended as part of the shape design.) $250-600.

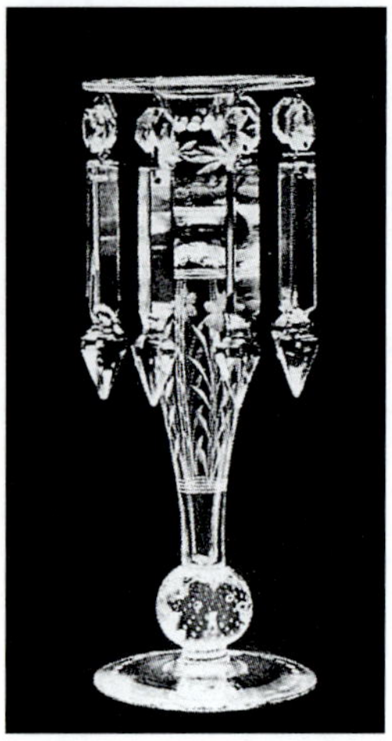

CANDLESTICK #B-1617, engraved in the CLARINA pattern, 10" h with (8) 5" spear prisms. (The prisms were intended as part of the shape design.) *Illustration from a Pairpoint Catalog*. $300-550.

CANDLESTICK #B-1628, engraved in the DEW DROP DESIGN, No. 218, 12" h. (This shape is most often found with (8) 5" spear prisms.) *Illustration from a Pairpoint Catalog*. $300-550.

CANDLESTICK #B-1626, engraved in the DEW DROP DESIGN, No. 218, 8.50" h. *Illustration from a Pairpoint Catalog*. $150-275.

CANDLESTICK #1629, engraved in the HAMPTON pattern, 10" h. *Illustration from a Pairpoint Catalog*. $250-450.

CANDLESTICK #B-1627, Black Amethyst, 9" h, (10.5" h), 12.5" h. $175-350.

CANDLESTICK #B-1634, Canaria, 9.25" h with (8) 4" blunt prisms. (The prisms were intended as part of the shape design.) $275-550.

CANDLESTICK #1635, Clear, engraved in the NOTTINGHAM pattern, 7.50" h. $200-400.

CANDLESTICK #1640, Green, engraved in the UNKNOWN "B" pattern, 5" h. (This shape will have a ground and polished bottom edge and no pontil mark.) $175-300.

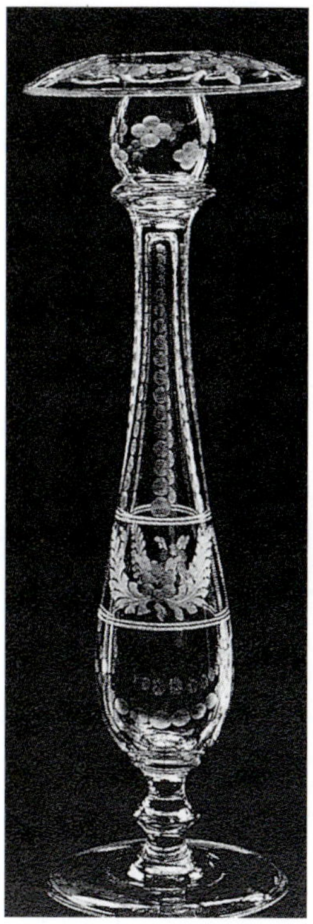

CANDLESTICK #1641, engraved in the ROCKFORD pattern, (12" h), 14" h. (This shape will also be found with a square foot.) *Illustration from a Pairpoint Catalog.* $225-550.

CANDLESTICK #1642, Black Amethyst & Clear, 4" h. (This shape will have a ground and polished bottom edge and no pontil mark.) $125-250.

CANDLESTICK #B-1811, Amethyst, engraved in the WEXFORD pattern, 12" h. (This shape will regularly be found with (8) 5" spear prisms, but not always.) $250-550.

CANDLESTICK #1811, Green, 12" h. $200-425.

CANDLESTICK # Unknown 09, engraved in the BOSWELL pattern, 6" h. *Illustration from a Pairpoint Catalog*. $125-250.

CANDLESTICK # Unknown 10, Canaria, 4" h. (The bubble ball on this shape will occasionally be found in a somewhat flattened configuration.) $100-225.

CANDLESTICK # Unknown 11, Cobalt Blue, 10" h. (This shape is commonly found in Clear with colored edges and threading—See Special Products chapter, "Colored Edge and Trim".) $200-450.

CANDLESTICK # Unknown 12, Canaria, 9.75" h. (This shape is intended to use the hollow ball connector. Therefore, no premium pricing will apply due to the hollow ball feature.) Occasionally this shape will be seen with a clear bubble ball connector instead of the same-color hollow ball. $200-450.

CANDLESTICK # Unknown 13, Rosaria, 10.50" h with (8) 5" spear prisms. (This shape is more commonly found without prisms.) $225-500.

CANDLESTICK # Unknown 14, Cobalt Blue, 5" h. $100-225.

LEFT: CANDELABRUM/2-LIGHT # Unknown 81, engraved in the HARWICH pattern, 10.50" high with a spread of 13". (This candelabrum was totally mold-formed and beautifully constructed of several pieces. Pairpoint, as well as Hawkes, purchased these blanks from the A.H.Heisey & Company (Heisey #301) during the early 1930s, and applied their own engraving patterns. This allowed Pairpoint to fill-out their candlestick line since they did very little mold-formed work of their own.) *Illustration from a Pairpoint Catalog.* $850.
RIGHT: CANDELABRUM/3-LIGHT # Unknown 82, engraved in the HARWICH pattern, 15.50" high with a spread of 13". (This candelabrum was totally mold-formed and beautifully constructed of several pieces. Pairpoint, as well as Hawkes, purchased these blanks from the A.H.Heisey & Company (Heisey #301) during the early 1930s, and applied their own engraving patterns. This allowed Pairpoint to fill-out their candlestick line since they did very little mold-formed work of their own.) *Illustration from a Pairpoint Catalog.* $950.

CANDLESTICK # Unknown 15, engraved in the UNKNOWN "F" pattern, 3.50" h. $100-225.

Opposite page:
TALL CANDELABRUM/2-LIGHT # Unknown 83, engraved in the UNKNOWN "M" pattern, 16" high with a spread of 13". This candelabrum is a tall version of Candelabrum # Unknown 81, but has *not* been found referenced in any old Pairpoint catalog pages. Likewise, the decorating pattern we have identified as UNKNOWN "M" has not been found; in fact the style of the decoration is more reminiscent of Hawkes' work. It is known that, along with Pairpoint, Hawkes purchased these candelabra from A.H.Heisey & Company (Heisey #300). Although a Pairpoint attribution on this tall version is questionable, we think it is very likely that consumer demand would have prompted Pairpoint to purchase some from Heisey and apply their HARWICH decorating pattern. *The Frost Collection (recently acquired from the collection of Diana Courtney and Stephen Moss).* $900.

CANDELABRUM/3-LIGHT # Unknown 84 . (It is very likely that this candelabrum was purchased from the A.H.Heisey & Company, as Pairpoint did very little mold-formed work.) *Illustration from a Pairpoint Catalog.* $350.

Comports or Compotes

The price ranges shown in the captions for each photograph or illustration refer only to the specific shape shown, without decoration. If the item shown includes some form of decoration, it is just happenstance, and should not be considered as a contributing element to the price range.

COMPORT #A-104, Amethyst, engraved in the GRAPES pattern, 6" d x __" h, (8" d x 4.25" h), 10" d x 5" h, 12.50" d x 5.50" h. $150-450.

COMPORT #A-215, Clear, cut in the Brilliant-era BALTIC pattern, 5" d x 6.75" h. *From the collection of Mary Cipolla*. $150-350.

COMPORT #A-198, engraved in the CORONAL pattern with festooning, 7" d x 8" h. *Illustration from a Pairpoint Catalog*. $175-450.

COMPORT #A-199, engraved in the SIRIUS pattern. *Illustration from a Pairpoint Catalog*. $150-450.

COMPORT #A-228, Cobalt Blue, engraved in the GRAPES pattern, 6" d x 3.75" h, 7" d x 4" h, (8" d x 4.50" h), 10" d x 4.75" h. $175-350.

COMPORT #A-210, engraved in the ENGLISH pattern, 6.50" d x __" h, (7.50" d x __" h), 8.50" d x __" h. *Illustration from a Pairpoint Catalog*. $175-475.

COMPORT #B-228, Emerald Green, 6" d x 4.375" h, (8" d x 4.75" h). $200-375.

OVAL COMPORT #A-239, Cobalt Blue, 3.5" long, 4.25" long, (5.25" long), 6.75" long. Expect to find this shape with both a polished pontil *and* a ground and polished top edge. $125-300.

COMPORT #A-278, cut/engraved in the MURILLO pattern, __" d x __" h, (7" d x 6" h), __" d x __" h. $150-375.

COMPORT #A-258, cut in the Brilliant-era pattern Uncatena, 10" d x __" h. *Illustration from a Pairpoint Catalog*. $275-700.

COMPORT #A-294, Green, cut in the ADELAIDE pattern, 5.50"d x __" h, 6.50" d x 6" h, (7" d x 6.50" h), 8.50" d x 7.50" h. $175-350.

COMPORT #A-299, engraved in the GRAPES pattern, 4.50" d x __" h, (8" d x 7" h), 9" d x __" h. It would not be unusual to find widely spaced vertical optic ribbing within the bowl area. *Illustration from a Pairpoint Catalog*. $175-400.

COMPORT #298, engraved in the ARBUTUS pattern, 3" d, (4" d), 5" d. *Illustration from a Pairpoint Catalog*. $75-250.

COMPORT #B-366, Flambeau & Black Amethyst, 6.50" d x 6" h, (8" d x 7" h). $175-400.

COMPORT #B-367, Clear, engraved in the DEW DROP DESIGN, No.218, 8" d x 5"h. $175-400.

COVERED COMPORT #B-382, Marina Blue, 9" overall height. $200-550.

COMPORT #372, engraved in the NOTTINGHAM pattern. *Illustration from a Pairpoint Catalog*. $150-400.

COMPORT #B-372, Clear, engraved in the DEW DROP DESIGN, No.218, 7" d x 8.25" h. $175-425.

TALL COVERED COMPORT
Unknown 23, Clear, engraved in the WILTON pattern, 12" overall height. $225-600.

OBLONG COMPORT # Unknown 16, cut in the DUXBURY pattern, 9.50" l x 5.25" w x 5.50" h. *Illustration from a Pairpoint Catalog*. $300-700.

COMPORT # Unknown 17, Clear, engraved in the MAYFAIR pattern, 6" d x 5.50" h, (7.50" d x 6" h). $100-300.

COMPORT # Unknown 19, Clear with Rosaria edge band cut-to-clear, engraved in the DARLINGTON pattern, 8.50" d x 8" h. $250-550.

COMPORT # Unknown 20, Auroria, engraved in the GRAPES pattern, 8" d x 8" h. Due to the style of this shape, do not expect to find a bowl bump. $200-500.

Below:
COMPORT # Unknown 22, Clear, engraved in the UNKNOWN "D" pattern, 6.75" d x 5.50" h. $175-350.

COMPORT # Unknown 21, 7.75" d x 7" h. This shape incorporates applied glass threading for the length of the stem. Sometimes this shape is made of one color only, but more frequently it is found in clear, engraved, with colored edges and threading (see the Special Products chapter, "Colored Edge and Trim"). *An electronically enhanced sketch of a comport seen in Atlantic City, NJ.* $200-450.

Vases

The price ranges shown in the captions for each photograph or illustration refer only to the specific shape shown, without decoration. If the item shown includes some form of decoration, it is just happenstance, and should not be considered as a contributing element to the price range.

COVERED URN #A-292, Amethyst, engraved in the GRAPES pattern, 6.50" h, 7" h, (8" h)—measurements are to top of body. $250-550.

COVERED URN #A-295, Canaria, engraved in the GRAPES pattern, 6" h, (8" h)—measurements are to top of body. $250-575.

COVERED URN #A-297, engraved in the BUCKINGHAM pattern. 10.50" h to top of body. *Illustration from a Pairpoint Catalog.* $250-650.

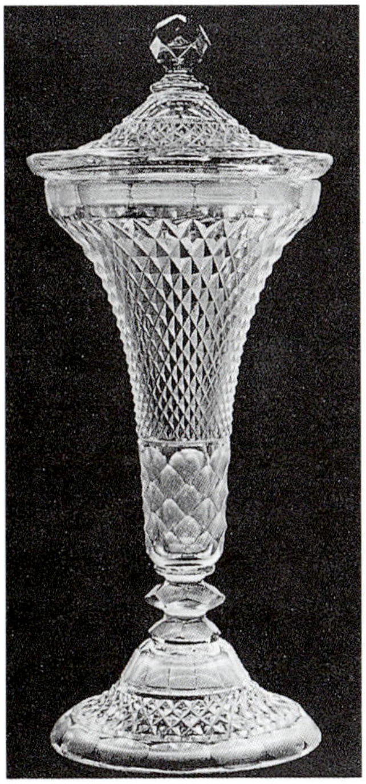

COVERED URN #A-298, cut in the ENGLISH pattern. *Illustration from a Pairpoint Catalog.* $300-750.

LUSTRE VASE #B-373, Green, engraved in the GRAPES pattern, 6.75" d x 11" h with (10) 6" spear prisms. $300-650.

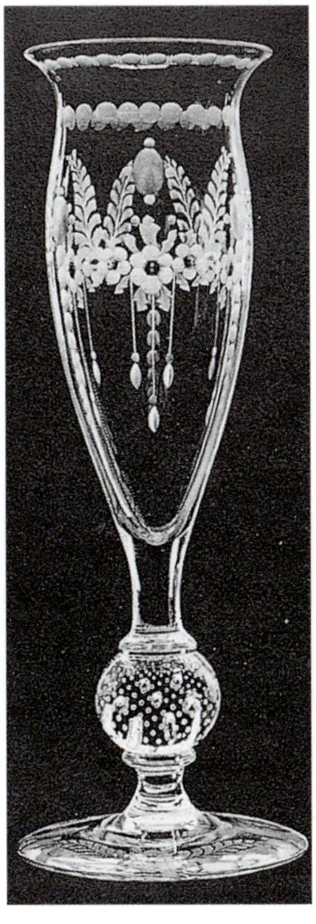

VASE #B-958, engraved in the DEW DROP DESIGN, No.218. *Illustration from a Pairpoint Catalog.* $200-550.

VASE #A-960, engraved in the COLIAS pattern. *Illustration from a Pairpoint Catalog*. $175-400.

VASE #B-960, Flambeau & Black Amethyst, 9"h, (12" h). $200-450.

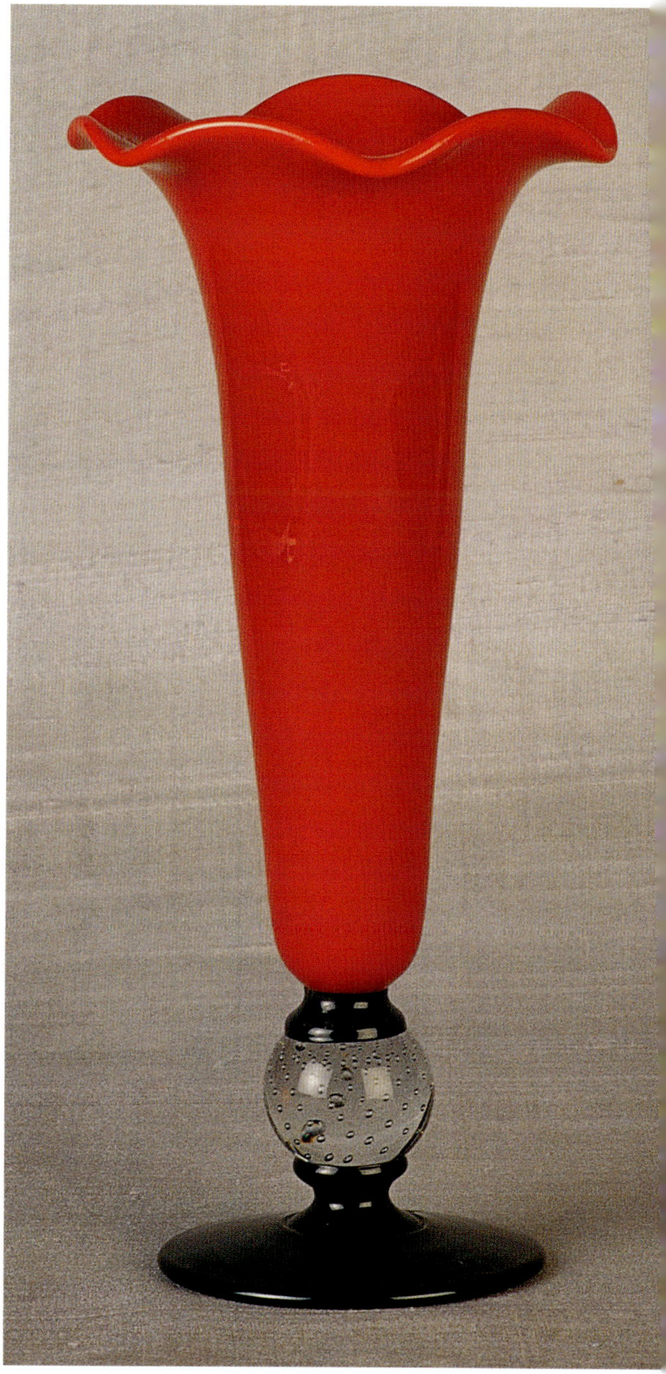

VASE #B-959, Canaria, 12" h. $200-450.

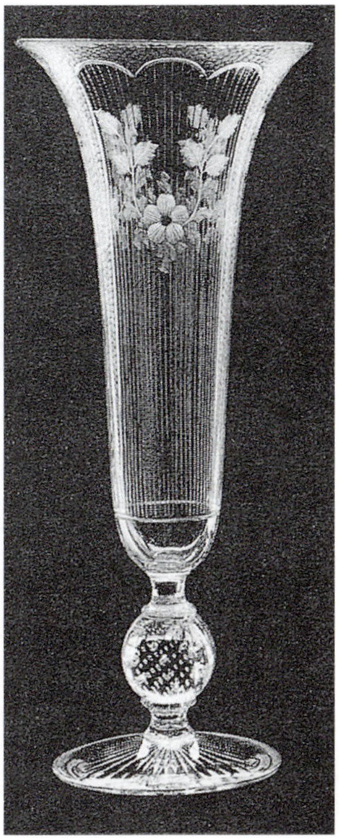

VASE #B-961, engraved in the HAMPTON pattern, 12" h. *Illustration from a Pairpoint Catalog.* $200-450.

VASE #A-1007, engraved in the CORNWALL pattern, 6" d x 6.75" h. (Available with a wire mesh flower screen insert which will increase the price to some degree.) *Illustration from a Pairpoint Catalog.* $150-400.

VASE #B-962, engraved in the DEW DROP DESIGN, No.218. *Illustration from a Pairpoint Catalog.* $250-550.

VASE #B-1007, Cobalt Blue, 8.50" d x 8" h. In the area where the bowl section meets the top of the bubble ball, there may occasionally appear a thin glass connecting wafer. $175-450.

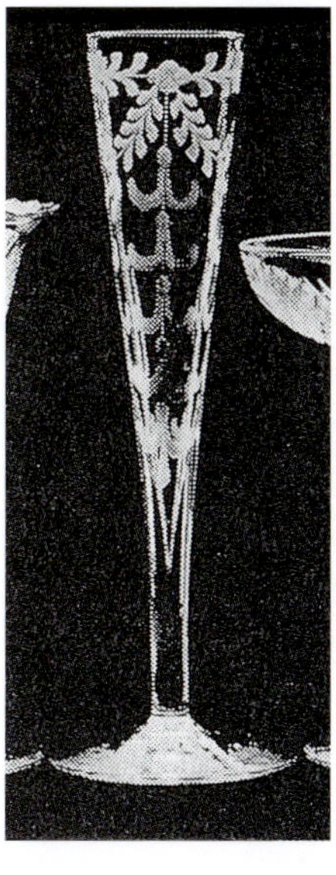

VASE #A-1018, engraved in the No.196 pattern. *Illustration from a Pairpoint Catalog.* $125-300.

VASE #A-1032, Clear, engraved in the UNKNOWN "G" pattern, 12" h. $150-450.

VASE #A-1034, engraved in the OSIRIS pattern, 6" h, (9" h). *Illustration from a Pairpoint Catalog.* $150-450.

VASE #A-1035, engraved in the NOTTINGHAM pattern. (Available with a wire mesh flower screen insert which will increase the price to some degree.) *Illustration from a Pairpoint Catalog.* $200-450.

VASE #A-1036, cut/engraved in the VISCARIA pattern, 8" h x 6.25" d. *Illustration from a Pairpoint Catalog.* $200-600.

VASE #A-1037, cut/engraved in the MURILLO pattern. *Illustration from a Pairpoint Catalog*. $200-525.

VASE # A-1038, cut/engraved in the VISCARIA pattern, 8" h. *Illustration from a Pairpoint Catalog*. $200-550.

VASE #A-1039, cut/engraved in the MURILLO pattern. *Illustration from a Pairpoint Catalog*. $200-525.

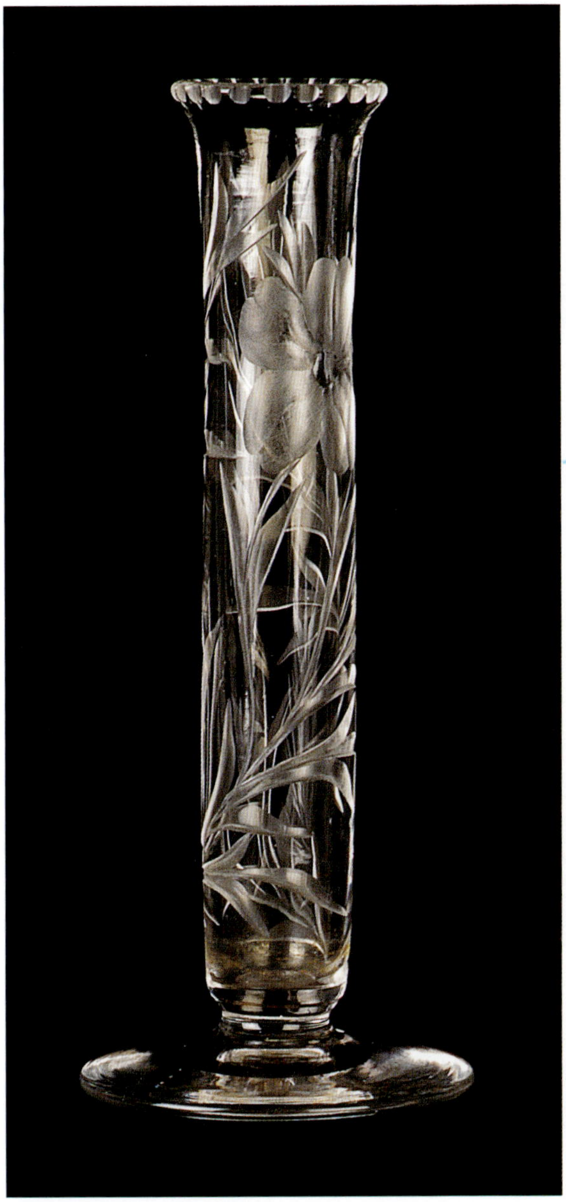

VASE #A-1045, Clear, engraved in the No.154 pattern, 6" h, 8" h, (10" h), 12" h, 14" h. $75-225.

VASE #A-1052, Clear, cut/engraved in the VISCARIA pattern, 8" h, (10" h), 12" h. $125-450.

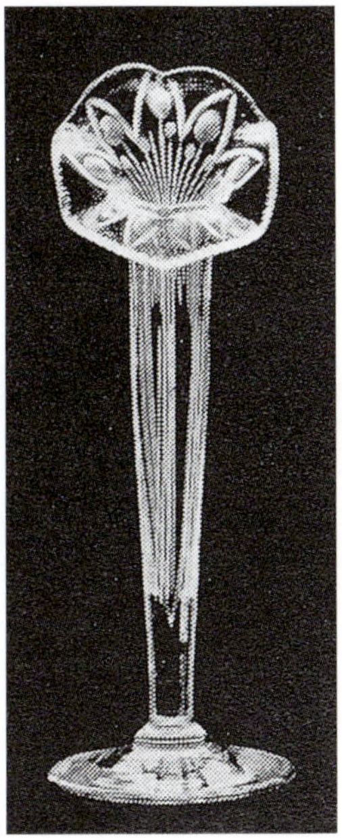

VASE #A-1046, engraved in the No.160 pattern, __" h, (__" h), __" h. *Illustration from a Pairpoint Catalog*. $75-225.

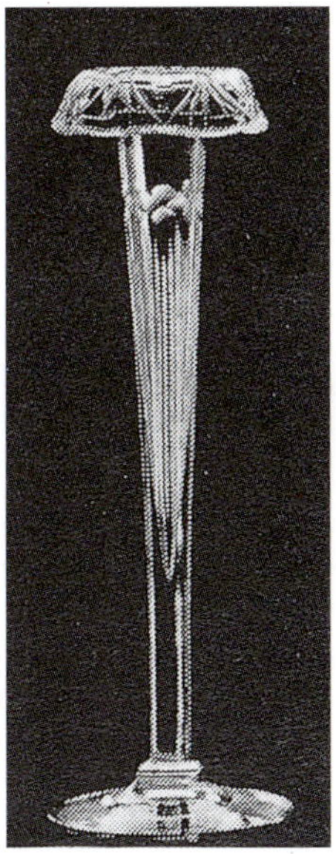

VASE #A-1053, engraved in the No.160 pattern, __" h, __" h, (__" h), __" h. *Illustration from a Pairpoint Catalog*. $75-225.

VASE #A-1055, engraved in the BUCKINGHAM pattern, 6" h. *Illustration from a Pairpoint Catalog.* $150-375.

VASE #1056, engraved in the GRAPES pattern, 12.50" h. *Illustration from a Pairpoint Catalog.* $175-450.

Left:
VASE #1060, engraved in the CLARINA pattern, __" h, __" h, (__" h), __" h. *Illustration from a Pairpoint Catalog.* $150-450.

VASE #A-1062, Green, engraved in the UNKNOWN "B" pattern, 6" h, 8.50" h, (10" h), 12" h, 14" h, 16" h. This shape was also available with two circular glass "drop" rings positioned near the bottom of the flared vase opening, about 1/4 of the distance down the vase from the top edge. These rings dangle from small circular glass mounting loops which were applied to the body of the vase during manufacture, and are not removable. The presence of the mounting loops without the dangling rings would significantly devalue the piece. $150-450.

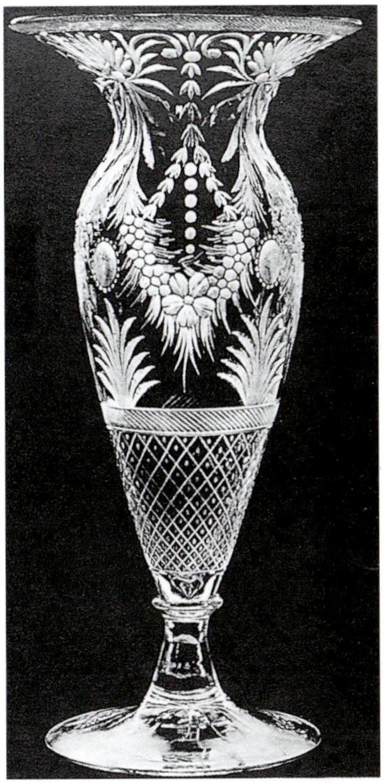

VASE #A-1063, engraved in the BUCKINGHAM pattern. *Illustration from a Pairpoint Catalog.* $175-500.

VASE #A-1064, Clear, engraved in the COLIAS (**) pattern, 12" h. $175-450.
**Note: This example is one of those anomalies that we cautioned you about earlier. For some totally unknown reason, the engraver omitted the spider web behind the butterfly (lucky for the butterfly). Otherwise the pattern is faithfully Colias.

VASE #A-1066, engraved in the BUCKINGHAM pattern. *Illustration from a Pairpoint Catalog*. $175-400.

VASE #A-1067, engraved in the CORNWALL pattern. *Illustration from a Pairpoint Catalog*. $175-500.

VASE #A-1068, engraved in the OSIRIS pattern, 8" h. This vase is also found *without* the glass drop rings. If this shape is found with the drop ring mounts, but the drop rings are missing, the value of the vase will be significantly reduced. *Illustration from a Pairpoint Catalog*. $150-425.

VASE #A-1069, Amethyst, engraved in the GRAPES pattern, 11.75" h. $250-600.

VASE #A-1072, engraved in the OSIRIS pattern, 9" h. *Illustration from a Pairpoint Catalog*. $175-475.

VASE #1070(?), engraved in the CLARINA pattern, __" h, __" h, (__" h), __" h. *Illustration from a Pairpoint Catalog*. $150-450.

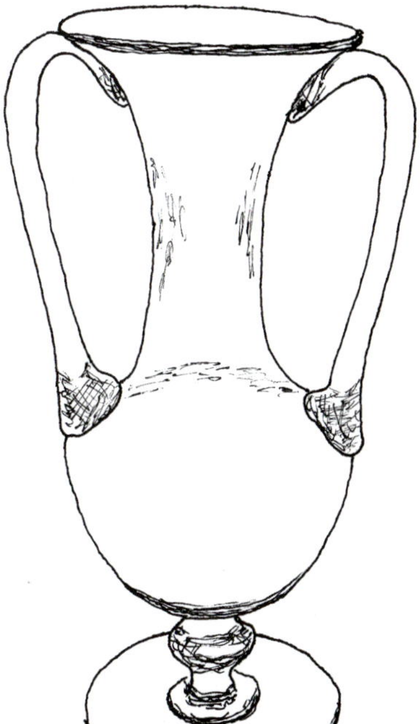

VASE #A-1070, 11" high. *Sketched from observation and electronically enhanced.* $250-600.

VASE #A-1073, Cobalt Blue, 6" h, (9" h). $175-475.

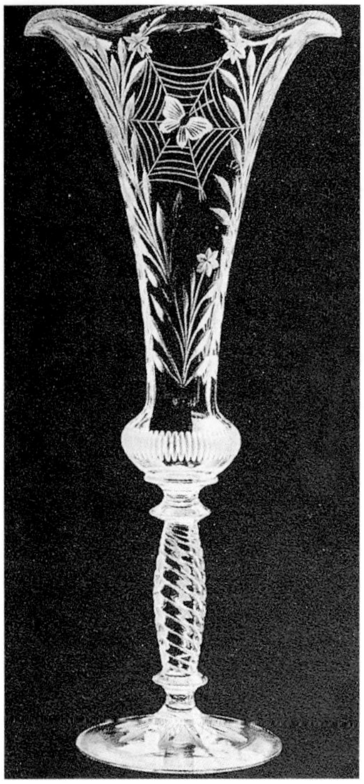

VASE #A-1074, engraved in the COLIAS pattern. *Illustration from a Pairpoint Catalog.* $275-600.

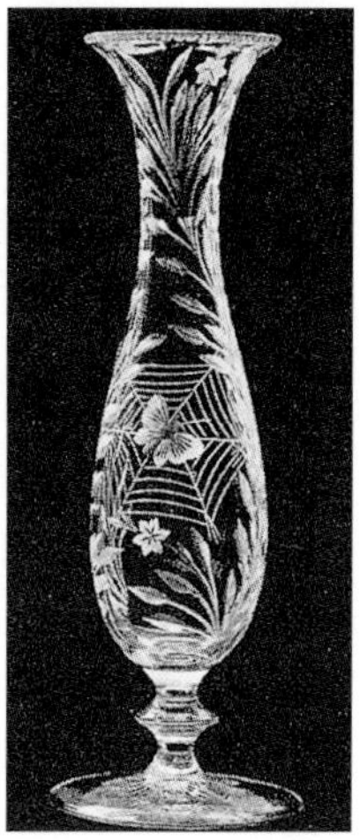

VASE #A-1076, engraved in the COLIAS pattern. *Illustration from a Pairpoint Catalog.* $175-450.

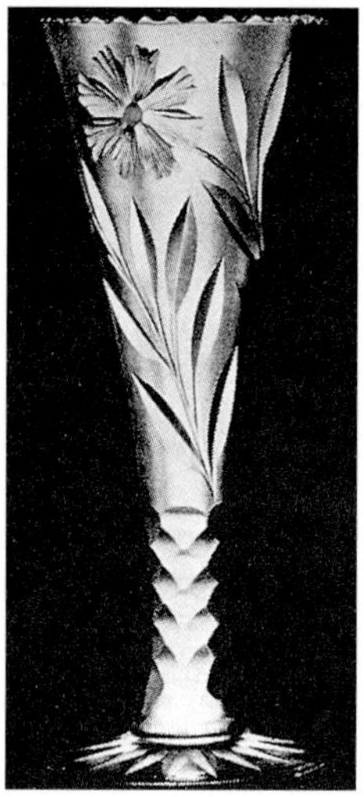

VASE #A-1080, cut/engraved in the VISCARIA pattern. *Illustration from a Pairpoint Catalog.* $150-400.

VASE #A-1081, engraved in the OSIRIS pattern, 10" h. *Illustration from a Pairpoint Catalog.* $200-500.

VASE #A-1075, engraved in the COLIAS pattern. *Illustration from a Pairpoint Catalog.* $250-550.

VASE #A-1077, engraved in the COLIAS pattern. *Illustration from a Pairpoint* Catalog. $250-550.

VASE #A-1078, engraved in the COLIAS pattern, 10.375" h. *Illustration from a Pairpoint Catalog.* $175-475.

VASE #A-1082, cut/engraved in the MURILLO pattern, 10.75" h with an oval-shaped opening 4.50" x 6". *Illustration from a Pairpoint Catalog.* $175-500.

VASE #B-1083, Cobalt Blue, 12" h. $225-600.

SWEET PEA VASE #1089, Clear, engraved in the GARLAND pattern, __" d x __" h, 6" d x 4.75" h, (8" d x 5.50" h), 10" d x 7.25" h. $150-450.

VASE #A-1099, engraved in the NOTTINGHAM pattern. *Illustration from a Pairpoint Catalog*. $200-500.

VASE #A-1100, engraved in the NOTTINGHAM pattern. (Available with a wire mesh flower screen insert which will increase the price to some degree.) *Illustration from a Pairpoint Catalog*. $175-450.

VASE #A-1084, Canaria, engraved in the GRAPES pattern, 12" h. $175-475.

VASE #A-1103, engraved in the NOTTINGHAM pattern. (Available with a wire mesh flower screen insert which will increase the price to some degree.) *Illustration from a Pairpoint Catalog*. $175-450.

VASE #A-1104, engraved in the NOTTINGHAM pattern. (Available with a wire mesh flower screen insert which will increase the price to some degree.) *Illustration from a Pairpoint Catalog*. $175-450.

VASE #A-1107, engraved in the NOTTINGHAM pattern. *Illustration from a Pairpoint Catalog*. $200-500.

VASE #B-1107, Marina Blue, (11.50" h), 13" h. $225-550.

VASE #A-1158, Clear, engraved in the BARRINGTON pattern, 8" h, (9.50" h), 12" h, 16" h. $150-425.

LUSTRE VASE #A-1164, engraved in the ROCKFORD pattern. (The prisms were intended as part of the shape design.) *Illustration from a Pairpoint Catalog.* $300-650.

VASE #1474, engraved in the GAINSBOROUGH pattern, 10" h. *Illustration from a Pairpoint Catalog.* $175-450.

VASE #B-1485, Flambeau & Black Amethyst with Sterling Silver Overlay, 13.25" h. $225-650.

VASE #B-1488, Clear, engraved in the DENMARK pattern, 12" h. $200-600.

VASE # Unknown 24, engraved in the COLIAS pattern. *Illustration from a Pairpoint Catalog*. $150-425.

VASE # Unknown 25, engraved in the DERBYSHIRE pattern, 10" h. *Illustration from a Pairpoint Catalog*. $200-525.

LUSTRE VASE # Unknown 26, engraved in the ENGLISH pattern. (The prisms were intended as part of the shape design.) *Illustration from a Pairpoint Catalog*. $300-650.

LUSTRE VASE # Unknown 27, Cobalt Blue, 11.50" h with (10) 6" spear prisms. (The prisms were intended as part of the shape design.) This vase was furnished with a silver-plated candle cup insert. Expect to find this shape with a ground and polished bottom edge and no pontil mark. $300-650.

LUSTRE VASE # Unknown 28, 11.50" h with (10) 6" spear prisms. (The prisms were intended as part of the shape design.) This vase was furnished with a silver-plated candle cup insert. *Illustration from a Pairpoint Catalog*. $300-650.

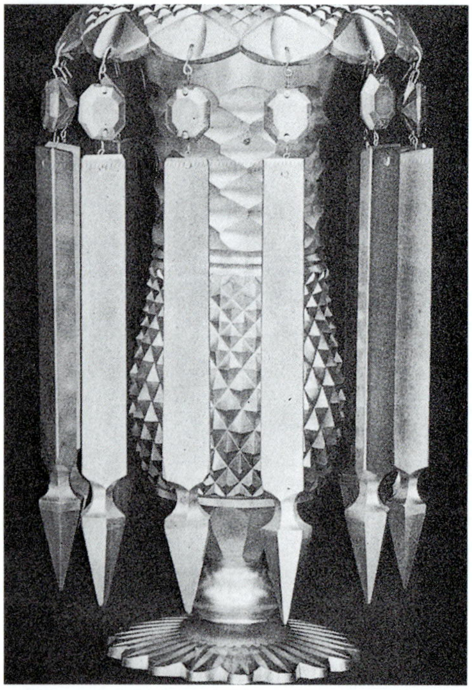

LUSTRE VASE # Unknown 32, engraved in the ENGLISH pattern. (The prisms were intended as part of the shape design.) *Illustration from a Pairpoint Catalog*. $300-700.

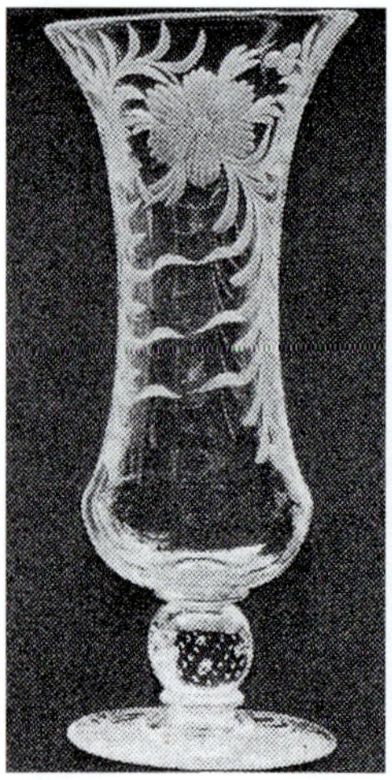

VASE # Unknown 30, engraved in the DENMARK pattern. *Illustration from a Pairpoint Catalog*. $175-450.

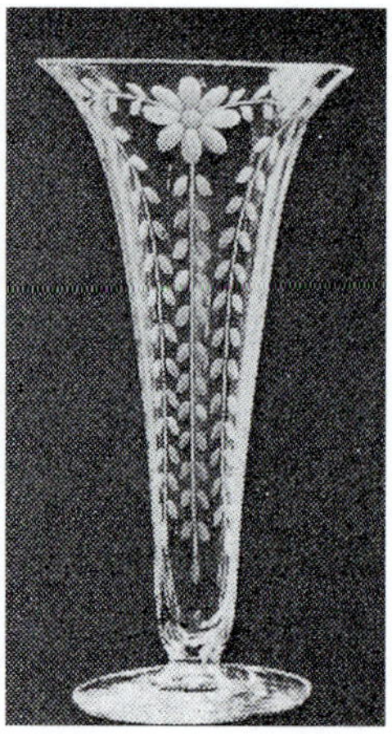

VASE # Unknown 31, engraved in the WREN Design. *Illustration from a Pairpoint Catalog*. $150-400.

CORNUCOPIA VASE # Unknown 35, Amethyst, 8.50" h. $125-400.

CORNUCOPIA VASE # B-2224, Clear, engraved in the WILTON pattern, 8.50" h. Although this vase is decorated in an early engraving pattern, it most likely dates to the Gundersen period (1939-1952). $125-400.

VASE # 2206, Ruby Red, (8" h), 10" h, 12.75" h, 14" h. This shape, most examples of which probably date to the Gundersen period, is occasionally found with a pair of applied curved loop handles located at the bulbous area on the lower portion of the vase. These handles, as well as the foot, may either be the same color as the body of the vase, or they may be Clear. This vase will also be found with a square base. $150-400.

VASE # Unknown 37, Ruby Red, 8" h, (10.25" h). This shape, most examples of which probably date to the Gundersen period, is occasionally found with a pair of applied curved loop handles located at the bulbous area on the lower portion of the vase. These handles, as well as the foot, may either be the same color as the body of the vase, or they may be Clear. It is also possible to find this vase with a square base. $175-475.

IVY VASE # Unknown 39, Amethyst, 12" h. $150-425.

VASE # Unknown 42, Cobalt Blue, 12" h. $200-500.

VASE # Unknown 43, Clear, cut/engraved in the VISCARIA pattern, 8.25" h. $125-350.

VASE # Unknown 44, 8.50" d x 8.25" h, (9" d x 10.75" h). *An electronically enhanced sketch of a vase seen in Torrington, NY.* $200-500.

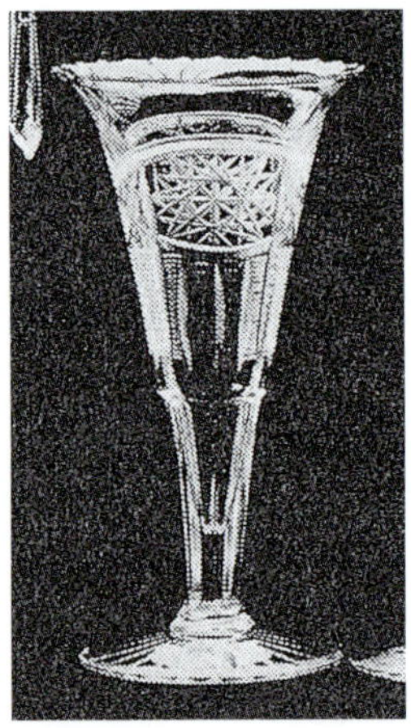

VASE # Unknown 80, unidentified Brilliant-era pattern. *Illustration from a Pairpoint Catalog.* $125-300.

Personal Items

The price ranges shown in the captions for each photograph or illustration refer only to the specific shape shown, without decoration. If the item shown includes some form of decoration, it is just happenstance, and should not be considered as a contributing element to the price range.

The items shown below are only a very small representation of the large variety of personal items made by Pairpoint. We doubt that anyone alive today has seen anywhere near the totality of these items. Since there were a multitude of undocumented shapes made, the best way to attribute a personal item to Pairpoint is to rely upon the decorating pattern. Fortunately for us today, Pairpoint decorated most of the blanks intended for personal use.

COLOGNE #14, engraved in the No.196 pattern, 1-oz. *Illustration from a Pairpoint Catalog*. $150-375.

Right:
COLOGNE #21, cut/engraved in the MURILLO pattern. *Illustration from a Pairpoint Catalog*. $200-450.

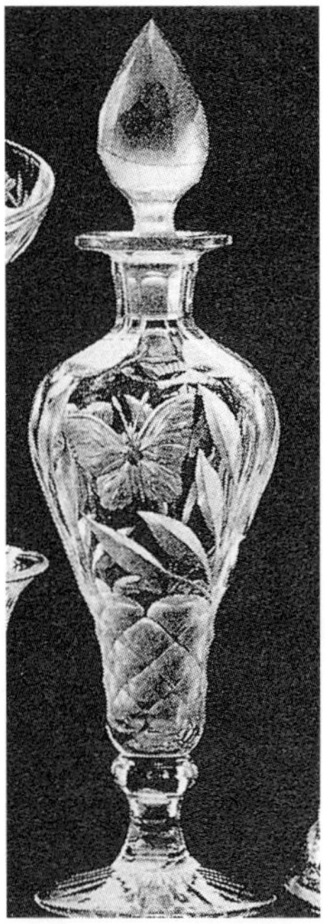

PERFUME #6, engraved in the No.136 pattern, 1-oz, (2-oz), 3-oz. *Illustration from a Pairpoint Catalog*. $175-400.

PERFUME #19, engraved in the No.136 pattern, 1-oz, (2-oz). *Illustration from a Pairpoint Catalog*. $175-400.

COLOGNE #8, engraved in the No.129 pattern, 1-oz. *Illustration from a Pairpoint Catalog*. $150-375.

COLOGNE #22, cut/engraved in the MURILLO pattern. *Illustration from a Pairpoint Catalog*. $200-450.

COLOGNE #26, engraved in the GARDENIA pattern, 1-oz, (2-oz), 3-oz. *Illustration from a Pairpoint Catalog*. $175-400.

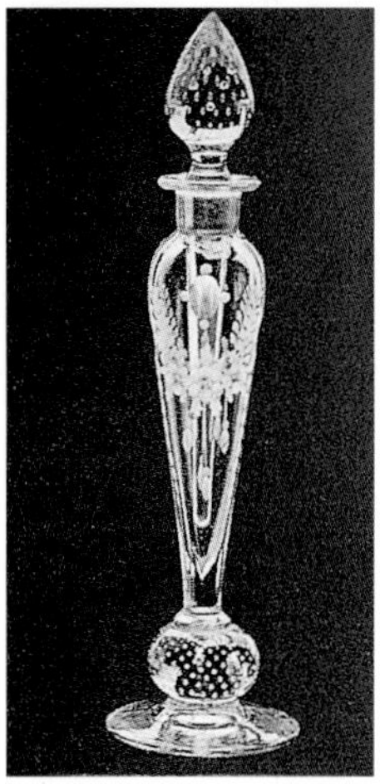

COLOGNE #B-31, engraved in the DEW DROP DESIGN, No.218. *Illustration from a Pairpoint Catalog.* $225-450.

NIGHT CAP SET (Bottle and Tumbler) #637, engraved in the CHELSEA pattern. *Illustration from a Pairpoint Catalog.* $250-600.

JEWEL BOX #4647/Small, #4648/(Medium), #4649/Large, cut/engraved in the VISCARIA pattern. *Illustration from a Pairpoint Catalog.* $275-700.

SMELLING SALTS JAR #546, cut/engraved in the VISCARIA pattern, small, (medium), large. *Illustration from a Pairpoint Catalog.* $150-350.

HANDKERCHIEF BOX #936, cut/engraved in the VISCARIA pattern, 6.75" square. *Illustration from a Pairpoint Catalog.* $275-700.

GLOVE BOX # Unknown 47, cut/engraved in the VISCARIA pattern, 4.50" wide x 10.75" long. *Illustration from a Pairpoint Catalog.* $350-750.

Serving Pieces and Bar Items

The price ranges shown in the captions for each photograph or illustration refer only to the specific shape shown, without decoration. If the item shown includes some form of decoration, it is just happenstance, and should not be considered as a contributing element to the price range.

The items shown below are only a very small representation of the large variety of serving pieces and bar items made by Pairpoint. We doubt that anyone alive today has seen anywhere near the totality of these items. Since there were a multitude of undocumented shapes made, the best way to attribute a serving piece or bar item to Pairpoint is to rely upon the decorating pattern. Fortunately for us today, Pairpoint decorated most of the blanks intended for entertaining, setting a table or outfitting a bar.

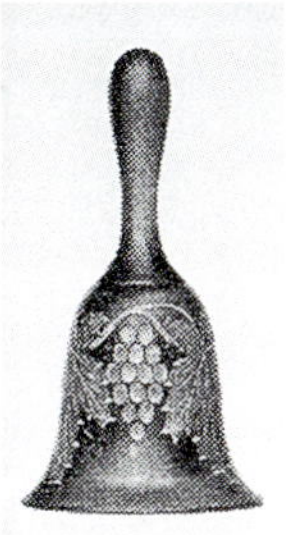

TEA BELL #1, engraved in the GRAPES pattern. *Illustration from a Pairpoint Catalog.* $150-350.

HANDLED PLATE #336, Clear, cut/engraved in the MURILLO pattern, 9.75" dia. $175-500.

GRAPE JUICE BOWL #138, engraved in the BUCKINGHAM pattern, 9" high. This bowl was accompanied by a varying quantity of #928 Juice Glasses and will frequently be found as a set. *Illustration from a Pairpoint Catalog.* $250-600.

PLATE #395, Green, engraved in the COLIAS pattern, 6", 8", 10", (12"), 14", 16" diameters. This shape appears to exhibit a smooth transition from side to side without any center depression or thickened central area. $125-400.

CRACKER & CHEESE PLATE (One Piece) #396, Clear, engraved in the WATERFORD pattern, 10" dia. This will have a polished pontil on both the top and the bottom. $175-450.

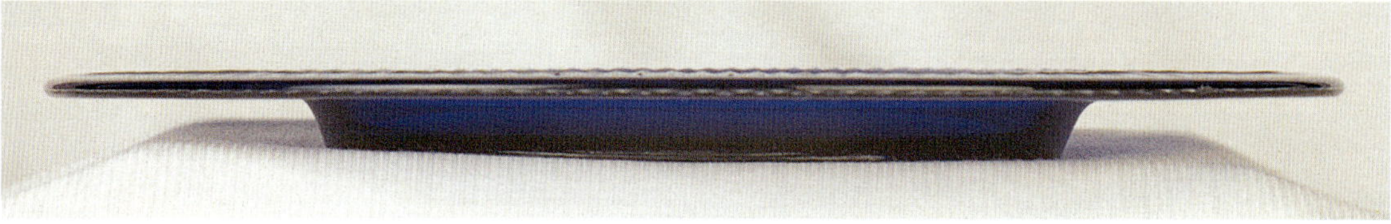

PLATE #397, Cobalt, 8.50", 9", (12"), 14", 16" diameters. This shape has a noticeable center depression and thickened projecting base area. $100-200.

SALAD PLATE # Unknown 65, engraved in the GRECIAN pattern. *Illustration from a Pairpoint Catalog*. $50-125.

FINGER BOWL UNDERPLATE # Unknown 66, Clear, engraved in the CORNWALL pattern. $35-75.

CELERY TRAY # Unknown 68, Clear, engraved in the BARRINGTON pattern, 4.50" wide x 10.75" long x 1.125" high. $75-250.

NAPPY # Unknown 69, Clear, cut/engraved in the MURILLO pattern, (5" d), 6" d. $75-300.

OVAL BOWL # Unknown 70, Clear, engraved in the BARRINGTON pattern, 6" w x 9" l x 1.75" h. $75-250.

TRAY # Unknown 71, Clear, engraved in the GARLAND pattern, 7" w x 10" l x 1" h. $100-375.

COVERED RELISH DISH # Unknown 77, Clear, engraved in the BLACKBERRY pattern, 9" d x 4" h. The lid is made of sterling silver, has the BLACKBERRY pattern engraved into the surface, and has a slot for the spoon. $150-350.

JUG #400, engraved in the GARLAND pattern. *Illustration from a Pairpoint Catalog*. $125-450.

Above right:
JUG #406, Clear, cut/engraved in the VISCARIA pattern, 2-pint. $125-450.

Right:
JUG #418, Clear, engraved in the ARBUTUS pattern, (3-pint), 4-pint. $125-450.

JUG # Unknown 75, Clear, engraved in the CLARINA pattern, 3-pint. $125-450.

JUG #457, cut/engraved in the VISCARIA pattern, 3-pint. *Illustration from a Pairpoint Catalog.* $125-450.

ICED TEA JUG #458, engraved in the No.151 pattern. *Illustration from a Pairpoint Catalog.* $150-475.

JUG #456, cut/engraved in the VISCARIA pattern. *Illustration from a Pairpoint Catalog.* $125-450.

JUG #459, engraved in the BUCKINGHAM pattern. *Illustration from a Pairpoint Catalog.* $125-450.

HANDLED JUG # Unknown 49, cut/engraved in the VISCARIA pattern, quart. *Illustration from a Pairpoint Catalog.* $125-400.

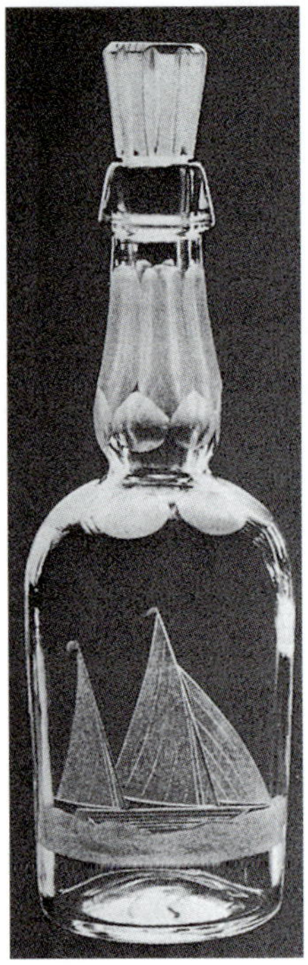

DECANTER #621, engraved in the SCHOONER pattern. *Illustration from a Pairpoint Catalog.* $100-350.

DECANTER #631, cut in the PUNTY AND RAISED DIAMOND pattern. *Illustration from a Pairpoint Catalog.* $100-350.

HANDLED JUG # Unknown 50, cut in the PUNTY AND RAISED DIAMOND pattern, quart. *Illustration from a Pairpoint Catalog.* $125-400.

DECANTER #627, cut/engraved in the VISCARIA pattern. *Illustration from a Pairpoint Catalog.* $100-350.

"DONUT" DECANTER #632, Cobalt Blue with hand-applied Sterling Silver Thistle decoration, 9" overall height x 6" wide. (This exact shape may be found in a small version referred to in an old Pairpoint catalog as #25-Cologne.) $250-600.

OIL #535, cut/engraved in the VISCARIA pattern. *Illustration from a Pairpoint Catalog.* $75-250.

DECANTER # Unknown 60, cut in the ADELAIDE pattern. *Illustration from a Pairpoint Catalog.* $100-350.

COCKTAIL MIXER w/EPNS Top # Unknown 64, engraved in the ROOSTER pattern, 2.50 pints. *Illustration from a Pairpoint Catalog.* $150-425.

CANDY JAR #B-915, engraved in the DEW DROP DESIGN, No.218, 8.75" overall height. *Illustration from a Pairpoint Catalog.* $150-400.

COCKTAIL MIXER with Silver Top # Unknown 61, cut in the ADELAIDE pattern. *Illustration from a Pairpoint Catalog.* $125-375.

BOTTOMS UP SET # Unknown 67, engraved in the CHELSEA pattern. *Illustration from a Pairpoint Catalog.* $200-500.

JUICE GLASS #928, Clear, engraved in the GRAPES pattern, 4.50" h. These glasses are used in conjunction with the Grape Juice Bowl #138. $50-100.

TUMBLER # Unknown 73, Clear, cut/engraved in the VISCARIA pattern, 1/2 pint. $40-100.

CANDY BOX #951, engraved in the BUCKINGHAM pattern. *Illustration from a Pairpoint Catalog*. $200-500.

PUNCH CUP #929, cut/ engraved in the VISCARIA pattern. *Illustration from a Pairpoint Catalog*. $60-125.

TOOTHPICK #1024, engraved in the No.129 pattern. *Illustration from a Pairpoint Catalog*. $40-125.

TOOTHPICK #1077, cut in the MITRE pattern. *Illustration from a Pairpoint Catalog*. $60-160.

TOOTHPICK #1025, engraved in the No.129 pattern. *Illustration from a Pairpoint Catalog*. $50-150.

ICE PAIL #1159, Green, engraved in the GRAPES pattern, (5.50" h), 7.50" h. This ice pail is fitted with an EPNS (electro-plated nickel silver) rim and handle and has an internal ridge near the bottom which supports an EPNS perforated drainer. A missing drainer disk would moderately devalue the item. $150-450.

SUGAR & CREAMER #1218, engraved in the CORNWALL pattern. *Illustration from a Pairpoint Catalog*. $150-375.

SUGAR & CREAMER #1230, Clear, engraved in the BARRINGTON pattern. $150-375.

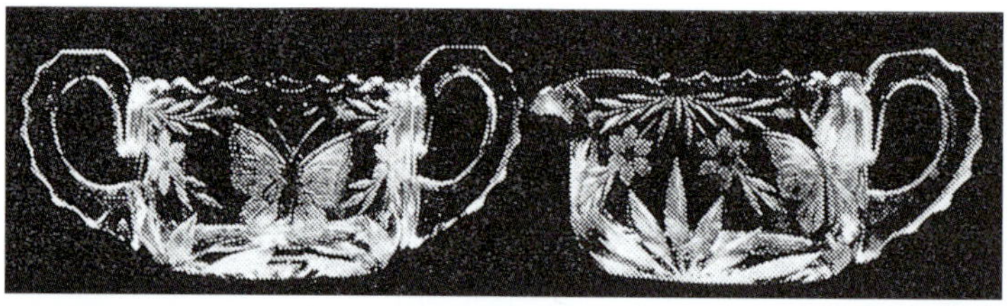

SUGAR & CREAMER #1255, engraved in the GARLAND pattern.
Illustration from a Pairpoint Catalog. $150-375.

SUGAR & CREAMER # Unknown 76, Clear, engraved in the CORONAL pattern with festooning. $150-375.

SMALL SYRUP #1502, cut/engraved in the VISCARIA pattern. The top is fitted with a silver-plated spout assembly. *Illustration from a Pairpoint Catalog*. $125-325.

JAM JAR #1654, cut in the Brilliant-era pattern Uncatena. *Illustration from a Pairpoint Catalog*. $60-175.

JAM JAR #1652, engraved in the No.192 pattern. *Illustration from a Pairpoint Catalog*. $60-175.

JAM JAR # Unknown 48, cut in an unidentified Brilliant-era pattern. *Illustration from a Pairpoint Catalog*. $60-175.

CIGAR JAR #1650 (25 cigar capacity), cut/engraved in the VISCARIA pattern, 6" h x 4.50" d. $175-500.
CIGAR JAR #1651 (50 cigar capacity), 7" h x 5.50" d. $225-550.
Illustration from a Pairpoint Catalog.

JAM JAR #1653, engraved in the No.195 pattern. *Illustration from a Pairpoint Catalog*. $60-175.

Stemware

The price ranges shown in the captions for each photograph or illustration refer only to the specific shape shown, without decoration. If the item shown includes some form of decoration, it is just happenstance, and should not be considered as a contributing element to the price range.

The items shown below are only a partial representation of the variety of stemware styles made by Pairpoint. Within each style line, Pairpoint produced the customary variety of shapes to accommodate anyone's choice of libation...goblets, clarets, wines, brandy & soda, cordials, cocktails, champagnes, etc. Since there were more styles of stems made than we can document for you here, the best way to attribute stemware to Pairpoint is to rely upon your recognition of the decorating patterns. Fortunately for us today, Pairpoint decorated most of their stemware lines. Another helpful factor in attributing stemware to Pairpoint (there are many look-alikes and wannabes) is to look for the existence of a polished pontil under the foot.

GOBLET #130, engraved in the BUCKINGHAM pattern. *Illustration from a Pairpoint Catalog.* $60-160.

GOBLET #140.5, engraved in an unidentified Vintage pattern. *Illustration from a Pairpoint Catalog.* $50-150.

GOBLET #150, engraved in the COLIAS pattern. *Illustration from a Pairpoint Catalog.* $50-150.

GOBLET #156, engraved in the OLD COLONY Design. *Illustration from a Pairpoint Catalog.* $50-150.

GOBLET #170, cut/engraved in the VISCARIA pattern. *Illustration from a Pairpoint Catalog.* $50-150.

SAUCER CHAMPAGNE #175, Clear, engraved in the Hempstead pattern. $40-135.

GOBLET #184, engraved in the WREN pattern. *Illustration from a Pairpoint Catalog.* $50-150.

COCKTAIL #1072, Clear, engraved in the BARRINGTON pattern. $40-140.

GOBLETS #5000, (Left) Green, engraved in the FLUTES & MITRE pattern, round foot. (Right) Clear, engraved in the UNKNOWN "K" pattern, square foot. $60-160.

GOBLET #5015, engraved in the TASSEL pattern. *Illustration from a Pairpoint Catalog*. $50-150.

GOBLET # Unknown 52, engraved in the GRECIAN pattern. *Illustration from a Pairpoint Catalog*. $50-150.

GOBLET # Unknown 54, engraved in the CAROL pattern. *Illustration from a Pairpoint Catalog*. $50-150.

GOBLET # Unknown 55, engraved in the OPERA pattern. *Illustration from a Pairpoint Catalog.* $50-150.

BRANDY & SODA TUMBLER # Unknown 57, Amethyst, engraved in the GRAPES pattern. $50-150.

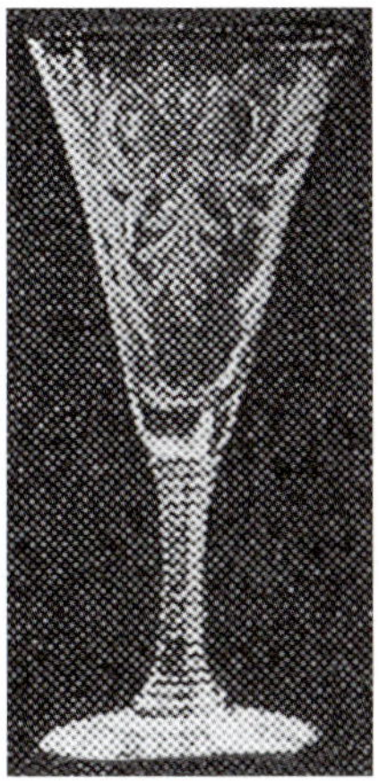

GOBLET # Unknown 56, engraved in the MORGAN pattern. *Illustration from a Pairpoint Catalog.* $50-150.

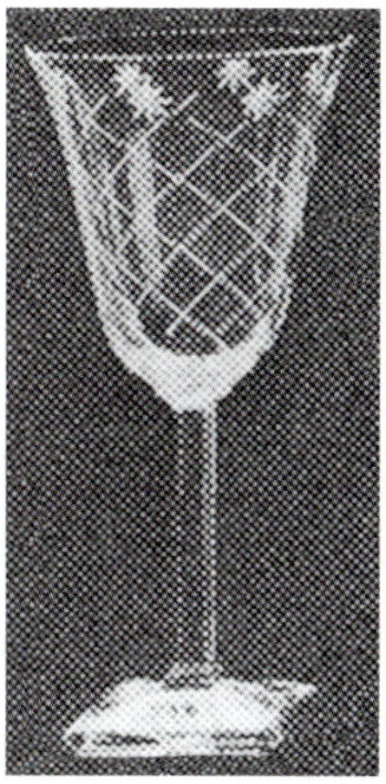

GOBLET # Unknown 62, engraved in the COMET pattern. *Illustration from a Pairpoint Catalog.* $50-150.

GOBLET # Unknown 58, engraved in the COBURN pattern. *Illustration from a Pairpoint Catalog.* $50-150.

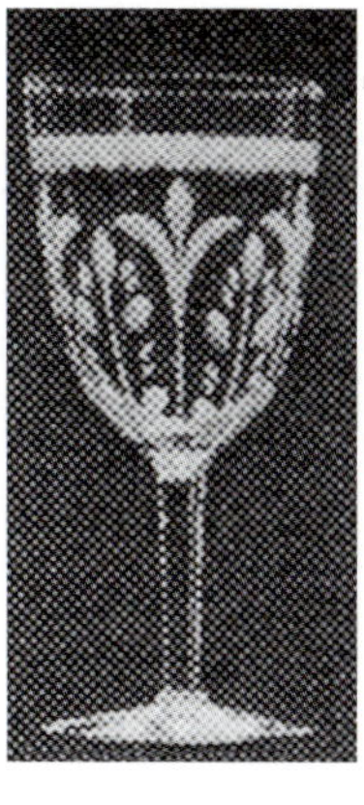

GOBLET # Unknown 59, engraved in the BARON pattern. *Illustration from a Pairpoint Catalog.* $50-150.

GOBLET # Unknown 72, Amethyst, engraved in the GRAPES pattern. $50-150.

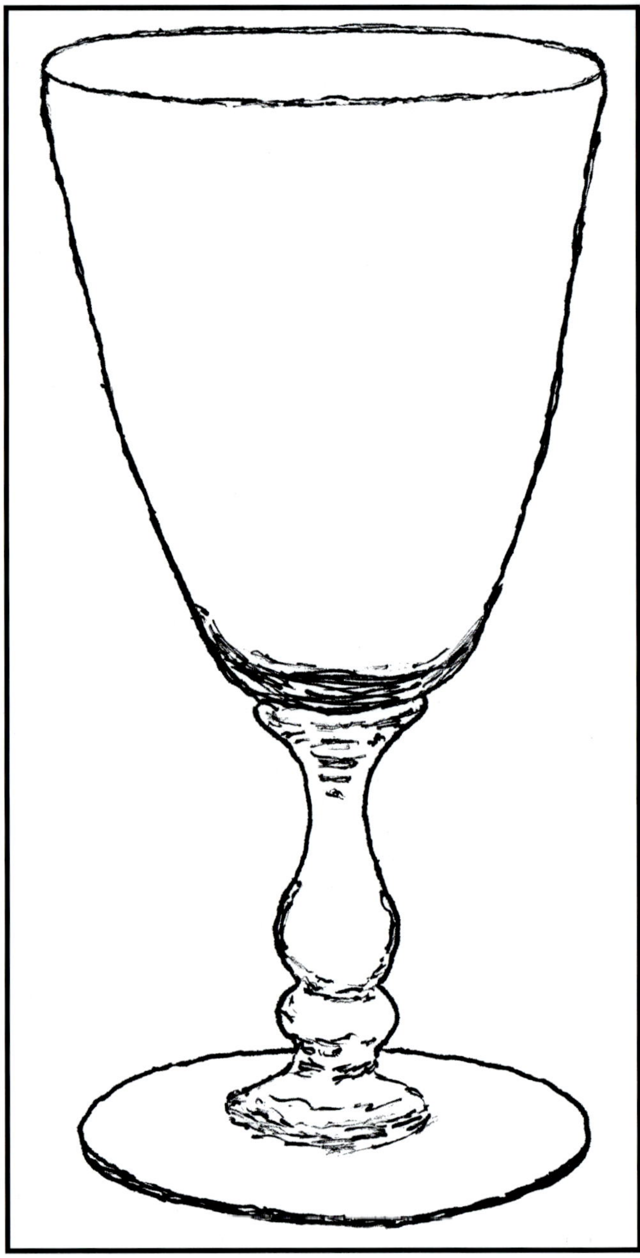

GOBLET # Unknown 74 . *Sketched from observation and electronically enhanced.* $50-150.

Miscellaneous

The price ranges shown in the captions for each photograph or illustration refer only to the specific shape shown, without decoration. If the item shown includes some form of decoration, it is just happenstance, and should not be considered as a contributing element to the price range.

The items shown below are only a very small representation of the large variety of miscellaneous items made by Pairpoint. We doubt that anyone alive today has seen anywhere near the totality of these items. Since there were a multitude of undocumented shapes and products made, the best way to attribute an item to Pairpoint is to rely upon the decorating pattern if it exists or some other feature that indicates a Pairpoint origin. Unfortunately, there are probably many Pairpoint items still around today that will never be properly attributed.

SMALL CLOCK #946, engraved in the GARLAND pattern, 5" h x 4" w. *Illustration from a Pairpoint Catalog.* $175-425.

LARGE CLOCK #947, engraved in the DAISY pattern, 8" h x 5.75" w. *Illustration from a Pairpoint Catalog.* $225-500.

DOOR KNOBS # Unknown 78 . $200-350.

Chapter 3

Decorating Patterns

Of all the skilled steps that went into the manufacture of Pairpoint glass, there were none that immediately and so overwhelmingly demonstrated the talents of the craftsmen as much as the surface decorating. Whether by stone wheel cutting, copper wheel engraving, or applied enameling, a fine glass form, which was beautiful on its own, was transformed into a magnificent work of art. It is our opinion that to truly capture the *essence* of Pairpoint glass one must see and think beyond the obvious. Certainly most people would agree that Pairpoint engravings are beautiful, but to go beyond the superficial beauty and to think about the process involved can only result in the development of a sense of awe and amazement. To think that a man could envision a design in his mind, transfer the rough layout to an ever-changing curved surface, then cut the design in a free-hand manner using various cutting wheels, and end up with perfect symmetry, alignment, and beauty is to give you a glimpse into something greater than man. In its own way, it is similar to viewing Itzhak Perlman's soul through the sounds of his violin. If you can allow yourself the freedom to experience the artisan's work at such deeper levels, only then can you capture the *essence* of the artform.

Before moving ahead into the particular characteristics of Pairpoint's surface decorating patterns, we would like to define some terminology that is constantly and incorrectly used by collectors and dealers. The regularly interchanged use of the words *cutting*, *engraving*, and *etching* certainly creates confusion whenever glass objects are discussed.

Cutting

This was the technique used throughout the Brilliant Period that resulted generally in deeper and wider geometric patterns being cut into the glass. Usually revolving stone abrasive wheels were used with the blank being positioned between the cutter and the wheel so that the cutter had to look *through* his blank to see his *work*. As the Brilliant Period came to a close, the demand for glass cutters diminished; the newer pattern designs were more figural and scenic with greater detail that could only be accomplished through the engraving technique.

An example of cutting from the Brilliant Period. This spooner was cut in Pairpoint's Malden pattern.

Engraving

This was the glass decorating technique that became the most common and fashionable as public taste evolved away from the heavy cuttings of the Brilliant Period. Often referred to as *copper wheel engraving*, the many shapes, sizes, and configurations of copper and other types of cutting wheels provided the means for the engraver to apply relatively shallow scenic and figural designs in minute detail to a thinner glass blank. In this process the engraver brought the glass blank up under his cutting wheel so that he would have a direct view of his work from above. By varying the depth of the pattern, three dimensional as well as textured effects could readily be achieved. It is generally agreed by most people who have an understanding of the two processes that engraving required a higher skill level than cutting.

Etching

Since this book is dedicated to the study of Pairpoint glass, we can eliminate the term *etching* from our operational vocabulary. Pairpoint simply did not decorate their products by etching. Their method of surface decoration, other than the occasional silver or enamel overlay, was by either cutting or engraving or a combination of the two. If you are discussing a possible Pairpoint item with someone, say by telephone or E-mail, and the other person says that the item has an etched pattern, you better clarify his definition of the term; if he really means *etched*, you can end the conversation right there; it cannot be Pairpoint!

A summary of the etching process will be helpful in differentiating the technique. Unlike cutting and engraving, discussed above, which involves the mechanical removal of the glass surface to achieve the design objective, etching is a chemical process. By applying a wax compound to the surface of a glass object in the *reverse* of the pattern desired and then exposing the unwaxed areas to an acid, the *unprotected* area would be *dissolved* or *etched* away, creating the desired pattern. There were generally two techniques used to apply the protecting wax to a glass surface. Either a *tissue*, which was pre-printed with the *reverse* of the pattern in wax, was applied to the blank and the wax transferred, or the blank was waxed all over with the design pattern exposed by removing the wax with sharp instruments. Depending upon the amount of time the unprotected areas were exposed to the acid, the depth of the pattern would vary. It has been our observation that the older and higher quality examples of etching work were deeper and better executed. Etching was used frequently on the better quality glassware of the Depression era and later, but never on Pairpoint glass.

As we thought about the general characteristics of Pairpoint's cutting and engraving work, we realized that the patterns speak for themselves. The only helpful thoughts that are not self-evident as you examine the photographs and catalog reprints have to do with accuracy and design element honesty.

An example of Pairpoint engraving on a #1159 Ice Pail. We have designated this unidentified pattern as UNKNOWN "C" .

This is an example of very high quality etching as found on a Dorflinger *Kalana/Pansy* Sweet Pea Vase.

This is an example of Pairpoint's Adelaide pattern decorating the bowl of a green comport. All of this cutting was accomplished by hand and shows remarkable consistency and accuracy.

Accuracy

By this term we are referring to the physical placement of the pattern on a glass blank as well as the *match-up* of the design elements within a pattern. The craftsmen were so skilled and talented that no matter how intricate a repeating design element was as it looped around and met itself where it started, they never ran out of space. You will never find any excessively *elongated* or *scrunched* element that was made to *fit* in that last open space. When examining a starburst cutting under a foot, you will see that all of the radiating lines that cross at the center actually *cross* at the center! When straight lines terminate at another line or groove, they actually *terminate* where they should...not early...not late. We have studied thousands of examples of all types of cut and engraved glass over the years; we have never seen better accuracy in design execution than we see regularly on Pairpoint items from the Middle Period.

Honesty of Design

This may seem to be a strange concept but it represents a very important factor that you need to know as you evaluate Pairpoint cutting and engraving patterns. Imagine for a moment that you are a designer of glass engraving patterns and have developed a concept for a new design. Perhaps you have drawn your design layout in a circular format such as could be replicated on a plate or open bowl. Then your supervisor, the Chief of Design, reviews your work and approves your design; but he also asks you to show him renditions of the design as it would look if it were applied to a candlestick or a vase. At Pairpoint, any design would be applied to any shape upon the request of a customer. You now have what some would call a *sticky wicket*. How could your pattern be modified to fit a totally different shape and contour that very possibly has much less surface area than the bowl or plate? If you worked for Thomas Hawkes or H. P. Sinclaire, you could rearrange your design elements, modify your design elements, or even eliminate some design elements that wouldn't fit into the space available. However, if you were a designer at Pairpoint, you would rearrange and modify your design elements in any way necessary to ensure that each element would be retained, regardless of the shape of the blank. This philosophy is what we call *Honesty of Design*. As you study the engraving designs on various glass items, you can rely on the retention of all the elements that the designer intended. They may be rearranged, maximized, minimized, or reemphasized, but all elements of the design will be there. If you come upon an engraved glass item that seems to have a pattern *close* to one of the examples in this book, in order for it to be Pairpoint's, close doesn't count.

Pairpoint was consistent in the *style* of their design elements. For example, the *butterfly* in the *Murillo* pattern is different from the *butterfly* in the *Garland* pattern. Flowers vary from design to design, vines change, and leaves have different textures, but...within any given design, the style and execution of each specific element is always the same! Train yourself to count the number of petals in a flower, the number and placement of spots on a butterfly's wing, the texture of a leaf, or the stems that connect the grapes in the *Grape* pattern, because *the attribution is in the details*. Pairpoint's *honesty of design* is virtually flawless.

In addition to the accuracy and consistency of each design element itself, you will find consistency in the method used to finish each element. Some general designs call for leaving specific design elements in their unpolished gray-cut state to provide contrast with the other elements that are polished. Whatever the designer's intention, any given design will always have the same finishing characteristics...always.

Using Motifs to Assist Pattern Identification

The following section provides a short-cut to the identification of Pairpoint decorating patterns. By identifying specific characteristics (arranged horizontally on the chart that follows) within any given pattern you are evaluating, you can follow the column vertically to determine all of the patterns that incorporate that characteristic. By checking multiple characteristics at one time, it will be relatively easy to see which patterns include all of the characteristics present within your example. Once a pattern has been selected for closer examination, the page number column will direct you to the photograph of that specific pattern.

		Flowers, Leaves, Vines	Butterflies aand Insects	Animals and Wildlife	Geometric	X's - O's - Y's	Fruits, Nuts, Berries	Cross-Hatching	Scenic	Grooves, Flutes, Facets	Fine Lines	Swags and Festooning	Panels and Vignettes	Bowties and Ribbons	Wheels & Spokes	Figural	Egyptian and Grecian	Cabochons & Punties	Brilliant Era-type Cutting	Fans	Fleur de Lis & Curlicues	Rim Pattern Banding
MOTIF PHOTO REFERENCE		A	B	C	D	E	F	G	H	I	J	K	L	M	N	O	P	Q	R	S	T	U
PATTERN NAME	PAGE NO.																					
Adelaide	125					X		X														X
Albemarle	125	X																				
Annette	125					X				X												X
Apples	125						X															
Arbutus	126	X	X																			
Ardsley	126	X																				
Asbury	126	X								X												X
Ashland	126	X									X											X
Baltic	127																		X			
Baron	127	X									X										X	X
Barrington	127	X																				
Beaumont	127				X			X														
Belvedere	128	X													X							X
Bingham	128	X			X	X						X						X				
Blackberry	128						X															
Bombay	128	X																				
Boswell	128	X																X				
Brilliant	129									X									X			
Buchanan	129	X						X					X								X	X
Buckingham	130	X						X				X						X		X		X
Burgoyne	130										X											
Carol	130	X																				
Chelsea	130	X										X										
Clarina	130	X									X		X									X
Cleveland	131							X													X	
Clyde	131				X	X												X	X			
Coburn	131	X										X										
Coleridge	131	X						X					X									
Colias	131	X	X																			
Comet	132							X														
Cornwall	132	X										X										X
Coronal	132				X						X	X										X
Daisy	132	X																				
Darlington	133	X						X				X										X
Delden	133							X													X	
Denmark	133	X																				
Derbyshire	134	X										X										
Dew Drop Design #218	134	X										X						X				X
Duxbury	134					X		X										X	X			

		Flowers, Leaves, Vines	Butterflies aand Insects	Animals and Wildlife	Geometric	X's - O's - Y's	Fruits, Nuts, Berries	Cross-Hatching	Scenic	Grooves, Flutes, Facets	Fine Lines	Swags and Festooning	Panels and Vignettes	Bowties and Ribbons	Wheels & Spokes	Figural	Egyptian and Grecian	Cabochons & Punties	Brilliant Era-type Cutting	Fans	Fleur de Lis & Curlicues	Rim Pattern Banding
MOTIF PHOTO REFERENCE		A	B	C	D	E	F	G	H	I	J	K	L	M	N	O	P	Q	R	S	T	U
PATTERN NAME	PAGE NO.																					
English	135							X											X			
Flutes & Miter	135									X			X									
Gainsborough	135	X																				
Gardenia	135	X									X											
Garland	136	X	X									X										
Gem	136	X																				
Gladstone	136	X						X				X										X
Glenmore	136					X		X											X			X
Gloucester	137							X					X									
Golfer	137															X						
Goodwin	137	X										X	X									X
Gothic	137	X											X		X							X
Graham	138														X						X	X
Grapes	138	X					X															
Grecian	138																X					
Guilford	138	X						X				X						X		X		
Hampton	138	X									X		X									
Hanover	139	X			X							X										
Harwich	139	X											X									
Hempstead	139	X																				
Hollow & Split	139					X				X								X	X			
Kent	140	X																			X	X
Kentwood	140	X										X										X
Lexington	140	X													X							X
Lincoln	141																	X	X			X
Lindfield	141	X						X									X					
Mansfield	141					X				X									X			
Mayfair	142	X																				
Melrose	142	X																				
Mitre	142									X									X			
Monroe	142					X		X											X			
Morgan	143	X																				
Murillo	143	X	X																			
Norfolk	143	X						X					X									
Nottingham	143	X						X												X		X
No.33	144									X									X			
No.129	144	X																				
No.136	144	X																				
No.151	144	X																				

		Flowers, Leaves, Vines	Butterflies aand Insects	Animals and Wildlife	Geometric	X's - O's - Y's	Fruits, Nuts, Berries	Cross-Hatching	Scenic	Grooves, Flutes, Facets	Fine Lines	Swags and Festooning	Panels and Vignettes	Bowties and Ribbons	Wheels & Spokes	Figural	Egyptian and Grecian	Cabochons & Punties	Brilliant Era-type Cutting	Fans	Fleur de Lis & Curlicues	Rim Pattern Banding
MOTIF PHOTO REFERENCE		A	B	C	D	E	F	G	H	I	J	K	L	M	N	O	P	Q	R	S	T	U
PATTERN NAME	PAGE NO.																					
No.154	145	X																				
No.160	145	X									X											
No.187	145	X										X										
No.192	146	X					X															
No.195	146	X																				
No.196	146	X																				
No.245	146	X									X	X										
No.246	147	X										X										X
No.247	147	X									X	X										
No.258	147	X																				
No.259	147	X																				
No.6280	148				X					X	X											
Old Colony	148							X														X
Opera	148				X	X				X												
Osiris	148	X															X					X
Patch Diamond	148									X									X			
Plymouth	149	X																	X			
Polar Bear	149			X					X													
Portsmouth	149	X						X				X	X									X
Princess	149	X											X								X	
Punty/Raised Diamond	150					X		X											X			
Richmond	150	X						X					X	X								X
Rockford	150	X									X	X			X							
Rooster	150	X		X																		
Royal Fern	151	X																				
Schooner	151								X													
Sirius	151	X	X					X					X									X
Spanish Galleon	152								X													
Staffordshire	152	X										X									X	
Strawberry Diamond/Fan	152							X											X	X		
Strawberry	152						X															
Tassel	153	X										X										X
Tyrone	153									X								X				
Viceroy	153																					
Victoria	154	X						X					X									X
Viscaria	155	X																				
Waterford	156	X										X		X	X							X
Wellington	156	X																				
Wexford	156	X												X	X							

		Flowers, Leaves, Vines	Butterflies aand Insects	Animals and Wildlife	Geometric	X's - O's - Y's	Fruits, Nuts, Berries	Cross-Hatching	Scenic	Grooves, Flutes, Facets	Fine Lines	Swags and Festooning	Panels and Vignettes	Bowties and Ribbons	Wheels & Spokes	Figural	Egyptian and Grecian	Cabochons & Punties	Brilliant Era-type Cutting	Fans	Fleur de Lis & Curlicues	Rim Pattern Banding
MOTIF PHOTO REFERENCE		A	B	C	D	E	F	G	H	I	J	K	L	M	N	O	P	Q	R	S	T	U
PATTERN NAME	PAGE NO.																					
Wickham	157	X										X										X
Wilton	158	X										X										
Windmill	158								X													
Wren	159	X										X										
Unknown "A"	159	X										X		X								
Unknown "B"	159	X																				
Unknown "C"	160	X																				
Unknown "D"	160	X										X										X
Unknown "E"	160	X																				
Unknown "F"	160					X		X														
Unknown "G"	161	X																				
Unknown "H"	161									X	X											
Unknown "I"	162												X					X				X
Unknown "J"	162	X																				
Unknown "K"	162							X		X									X			
Unknown "L"	163							X										X	X			
Unknown "M"	163	X																				
Unknown "N"	163	X																				

Illustrated Pattern Listing By Motifs

Photo References	Motifs
A	Flowers, Leaves, and Vines
B	Butterflies and Insects
C	Animals and Wildlife
D	Geometric
E	X's - O's - Y's
F	Fruits, Nuts, and Berries
G	Cross-Hatching
H	Scenic
I	Grooves, Flutes, and Facets
J	Fine Lines
K	Swags and Festooning
L	Panels and Vignettes
M	Bowties and Ribbons
N	Wheels and Radiating Spokes
O	Figural
P	Egyptian and Grecian
Q	Cabochons and Punties
R	Brilliant Era-Type Cutting
S	Fans
T	Fleur de Lis and Curlicues
U	Rim Pattern Banding

Motif **A**, the **Flowers, Leaves, and Vines** motif.

Motif **B**, the **Butterflies and Insects** motif.

Motif **C**, the **Animals and Wildlife** motif.

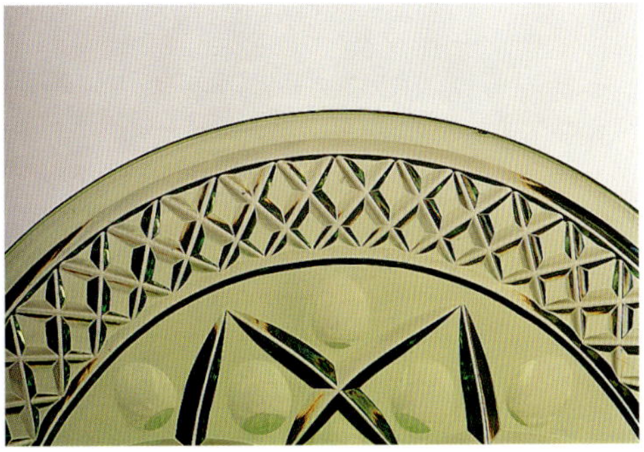

Motif **G**, the **Cross-Hatching** motif.

Motif **K**, the **Swags and Festooning** motif.

Motif **D**, the **Geometric** motif.

Motif **H**, the **Scenic** motif.

Motif **L**, the **Panels and Vignettes** motif.

Motif **E**, the **X's - O's - Y's** motif.

Motif **I**, the **Grooves, Flutes, and Facets** motif.

Motif **M**, the **Bowties and Ribbons** motif.

Motif **F**, the **Fruits, Nuts, and Berries** motif.

Motif **J**, the **Fine Lines** motif.

Motif **N**, the **Wheels and Radiating Spokes** motif.

Motif **O**,the **Figural** motif. *Illustration from a Pairpoint Catalog.*

Motif **R**, the **Brilliant Era-Type Cutting** motif.

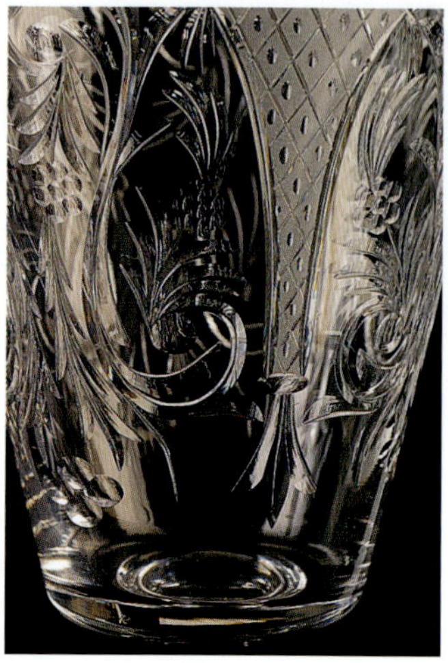

Motif **T**, the **Fleur-de-Lis and Curlicues** motif.

Motif **P**, the **Egyptian and Grecian** motif. *Illustration from a Pairpoint Catalog.*

Motif **S**, the **Fans** motif.

Motif **U**, the **Rim Pattern Banding** motif.

Motif **Q**, the **Cabochons and Punties** motif.

The Decorating Patterns

The majority of the engraving patterns applied by Pairpoint to their glass decorative and utilitarian products are alphabetically presented in the photographs that follow, but we know that more exist. The lack of reference material about Pairpoint glass is noteworthy, so we have had to rely upon our own travels and acquisitions to expand our information base. Naturally, without factory catalogs and sales sheets, any *new* patterns *discovered* can not be attributed to Pairpoint with an absolute degree of certainty. However, we have decided to trust our acquired sense of Pairpoint's style and physical characteristics to suggest an attribution to them. We have identified these undocumented patterns by using a letter code such as *Unknown "A"*. All of these patterns have been found on Pairpoint blanks, and in most cases they have been seen on more than one occasion. Hopefully, future information will come to light to verify our attribution...or refute it.

ADELAIDE pattern shown on a Green #A-294 Comport. DESIRABILITY SCORE = 4

ANNETTE pattern. *Illustration from a Pairpoint Catalog.* DESIRABILITY SCORE = 4

ALBEMARLE pattern shown on a #1072 Goblet. *Illustration from a Pairpoint Catalog.* DESIRABILITY SCORE = 3

APPLES pattern. *Illustration from a Pairpoint Catalog.* DESIRABILITY SCORE = 5

ARDSLEY pattern shown on a #B-1083 Vase. *Illustration from a Pairpoint Catalog.* DESIRABILITY SCORE = 5

ARBUTUS pattern shown on a Clear #406 Jug. DESIRABILITY SCORE = 4

ASHLAND pattern shown on a #B-1485 Vase. *Illustration from a Pairpoint Catalog.* DESIRABILITY SCORE = 4

ASBURY pattern shown on a 1/2 pint Tumbler. *Illustration from a Pairpoint Catalog.* DESIRABILITY SCORE = 2

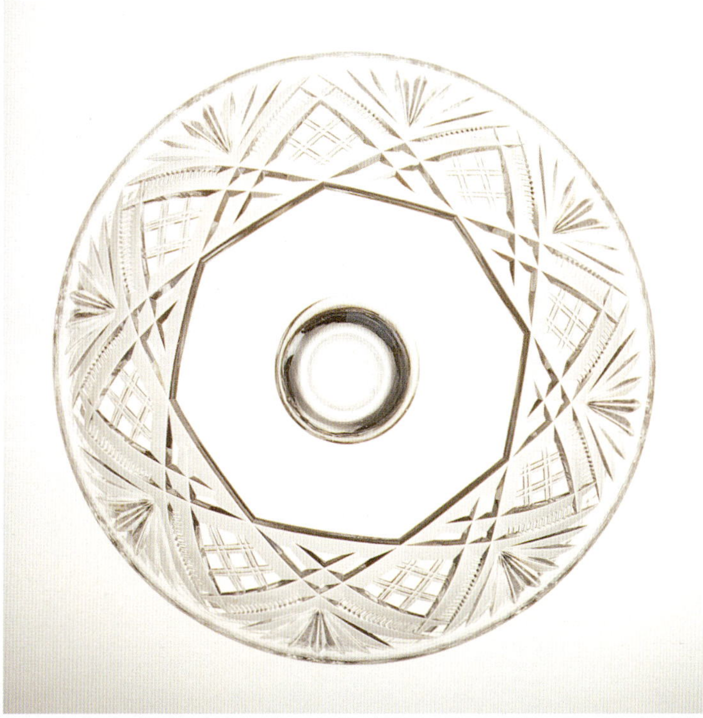

BALTIC pattern shown on a Clear #A-215 Comport. *From the collection of Mary Cipolla*. DESIRABILITY SCORE = 4

BARRINGTON pattern shown on a Clear #395 Plate. DESIRABILITY SCORE = 3

BARON pattern shown on a Clear #A-1062 Vase. DESIRABILITY SCORE = 3

BEAUMONT pattern shown on a Fine Arts Line Centerpiece #C5558. *Illustration from a Pairpoint Catalog*. DESIRABILITY SCORE = 5

BELVEDERE pattern shown on a Clear #A-194 Bowl.
DESIRABILITY SCORE = 4

BLACKBERRY pattern shown on a Green #A-294 Comport.
DESIRABILITY SCORE = 4

BINGHAM pattern. *Illustration from a Pairpoint Catalog.* DESIRABILITY SCORE = 3

BOMBAY pattern shown on a #A-249 Nappy. *Illustration from a Pairpoint Catalog.*
DESIRABILITY SCORE = 2

BOSWELL pattern. *Illustration from a Pairpoint Catalog.*
DESIRABILITY SCORE = 3

BRILLIANT pattern shown on a Clear #A-228 Comport. DESIRABILITY SCORE = 3

Above and left:
BUCHANAN pattern shown in two views on a Clear #B-1083 Vase. DESIRABILITY SCORE = 5

BUCKINGHAM pattern shown on a Clear #A-228 Comport. DESIRABILITY SCORE = 5

CHELSEA pattern shown on a Clear #395 Plate. DESIRABILITY SCORE = 3

BURGOYNE pattern shown on a # Unknown 61 Cocktail Shaker. *Illustration from a Pairpoint Catalog*. DESIRABILITY SCORE = 2

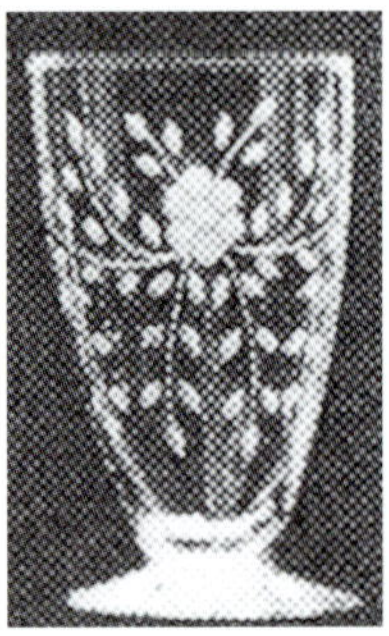

CAROL pattern shown on a # Unknown 53 Brandy & Soda Tumbler. *Illustration from a Pairpoint Catalog*. DESIRABILITY SCORE = 2

CLARINA pattern shown on a Clear #A-294 Comport. This pattern is similar to the Gardenia pattern and may be inadvertently confused. DESIRABILITY SCORE = 1

CLEVELAND pattern. *Illustration from a Pairpoint Catalog.* DESIRABILITY SCORE = 5

COLERIDGE pattern shown on a #A-194 Bowl. *Illustration from a Pairpoint Catalog.* DESIRABILITY SCORE = 5

CLYDE pattern shown on a # Unknown 61 Cocktail Shaker. *Illustration from a Pairpoint Catalog.* DESIRABILITY SCORE = 4

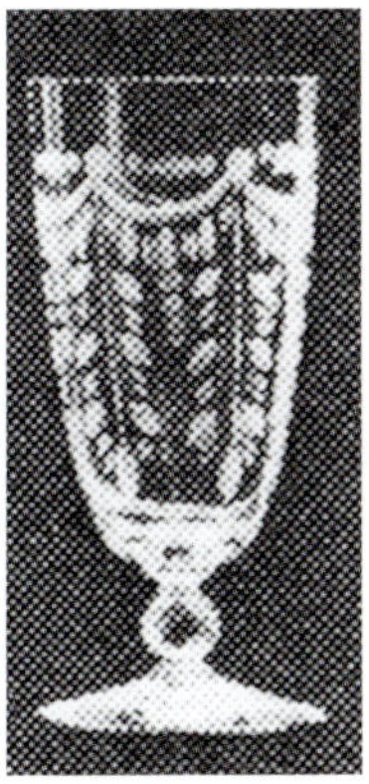

COBURN pattern shown on a # Unknown 58 Brandy & Soda Tumbler. *Illustration from a Pairpoint Catalog.* DESIRABILITY SCORE = 2

COLIAS pattern shown on a Green #395 Plate. DESIRABILITY SCORE = 5

COMET pattern shown on a # Unknown 62 Brandy and Soda Tumbler. *Illustration from a Pairpoint Catalog*. DESIRABILITY SCORE = 1

CORNWALL pattern shown on a Clear Finger Bowl Underplate. DESIRABILITY SCORE = 4

CORONAL (with Festooning) pattern shown on a Clear #A-228 Comport. This pattern may occasionally be found without the floral swag (festooning). DESIRABILITY SCORE = 4

DAISY pattern shown on a #947 Clock. This pattern can be difficult to identify because of the similarity of the Daisy flower to flowers cut by other companies. Be sure to count the number of petals (16) and observe the texture detail of the petals and flower center. *Illustration from a Pairpoint Catalog*. DESIRABILITY SCORE = 3

DARLINGTON pattern shown on a Rosaria-banded Clear # Unknown 19 Comport. This pattern is virtually identical to the Gladstone pattern except for the cross-hatching in the cut-to-clear rim banding. DESIRABILITY SCORE = 5

DELDEN pattern shown on the glass portion of a Fine Arts Line Cigarette Holder. DESIRABILITY SCORE = 3

DENMARK pattern shown on a Clear #B-1488 Vase. DESIRABILITY SCORE = 3

DERBYSHIRE pattern shown on a # Unknown 25 Vase. *Illustration from a Pairpoint Catalog.* DESIRABILITY SCORE = 5

DEW DROP DESIGN, No.218 pattern shown on a Clear #B-369 Centerpiece Bowl. There are similarities between this pattern and the engraving pattern that always appears on the Venetti Design items (see the "Special Products" chapter), but ultimately there should be no confusion. DESIRABILITY SCORE = 3

DUXBURY pattern shown on a console set made up of a # Unknown 16 Comport and #1641 Candlesticks. *Illustration from a Pairpoint Catalog.* DESIRABILITY SCORE = 3

ENGLISH pattern shown on a #4970 Fine Arts Line Cigarette Holder. It is worth mentioning that on many shapes this pattern is transitioned by the use of cut faceting to improve the overall *look* of the decoration. DESIRABILITY SCORE = 4

GAINSBOROUGH pattern shown on a #1474 Vase. *Illustration from a Pairpoint Catalog*. DESIRABILITY SCORE = 5

FLUTES & MITER pattern shown on a Clear #A-228 Comport. DESIRABILITY SCORE = 2

GARDENIA pattern shown on a #26 Cologne. This pattern is very similar to Clarina, and may be easily confused. *Illustration from a Pairpoint Catalog*. DESIRABILITY SCORE = 2

GARLAND pattern shown on a Clear #358 Tray. DESIRABILITY SCORE = 4

GLADSTONE pattern shown on the Clear lid of a #B-382 Covered Comport. This pattern is extremely similar to the Darlington pattern, which has a different rim band design. DESIRABILITY SCORE = 5

GEM pattern shown on a (L) #1319 Salt and a (R) #1318 Salt. *Illustration from a Pairpoint Catalog.* DESIRABILITY SCORE = 1

GLENMORE pattern shown on a Clear # Unknown 03 Bowl. DESIRABILITY SCORE = 4

GLOUCESTER pattern shown on a #5000 Goblet. *Illustration from a Pairpoint Catalog.* DESIRABILITY SCORE = 3

GOODWIN pattern shown on a #1158 Vase. *Illustration from a Pairpoint Catalog.* DESIRABILITY SCORE = 4

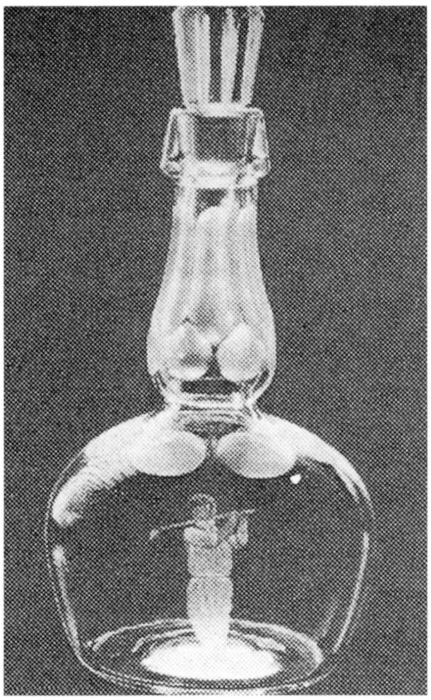

GOLFER pattern shown on a #631 Decanter. *Illustration from a Pairpoint Catalog.* DESIRABILITY SCORE = 5

GOTHIC pattern. *Illustration from a Pairpoint Catalog.* DESIRABILITY SCORE = 5

GRAHAM pattern. *Illustration from a Pairpoint Catalog.* DESIRABILITY SCORE = 5

GRECIAN pattern shown on a # Unknown 52 Brandy & Soda Tumbler. *Illustration from a Pairpoint Catalog.* DESIRABILITY SCORE = 2

GUILFORD pattern shown on a #1072 Goblet. *Illustration from a Pairpoint Catalog.* DESIRABILITY SCORE = 5

GRAPES pattern shown on an Auroria # Unknown 20 Comport. Look for the grape "stems". DESIRABILITY SCORE = 5

HAMPTON pattern shown on a Clear # Unknown 02 Bowl. DESIRABILITY SCORE = 5

HANOVER pattern. *Illustration from a Pairpoint Catalog.* DESIRABILITY SCORE = 4

HEMPSTEAD pattern shown on a Clear #175 Saucer Champagne. DESIRABILITY SCORE = 4

HARWICH pattern shown on the foot of a # Unknown 81 Candelabrum. *Illustration from a Pairpoint Catalog.* DESIRABILITY SCORE = 3

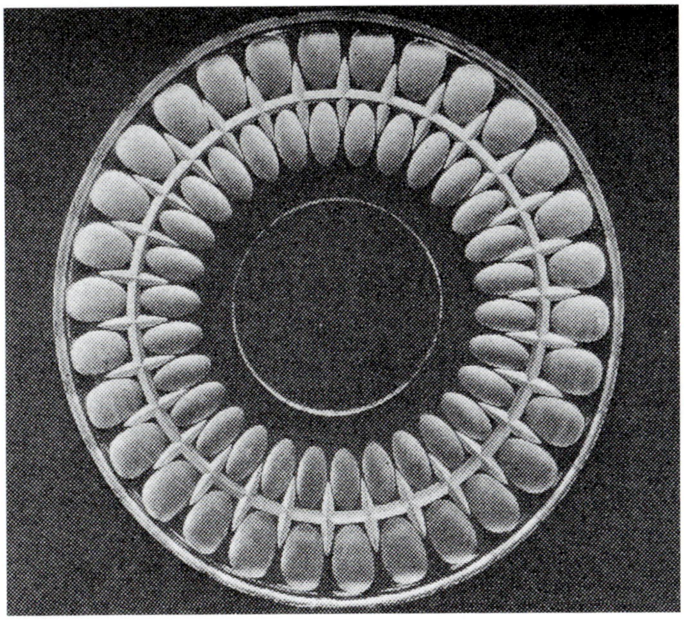

HOLLOW & SPLIT pattern. *Illustration from a Pairpoint Catalog.* DESIRABILITY SCORE = 4

KENT pattern. *Illustration from a Pairpoint Catalog.* DESIRABILITY SCORE = 5

KENTWOOD pattern shown on a Clear #A-194 Bowl. DESIRABILITY SCORE = 5

LEXINGTON pattern. *Illustration from a Pairpoint Catalog.* DESIRABILITY SCORE = 5

LINCOLN pattern shown on a Rosaria cut-to-clear #B-1485 Vase. DESIRABILITY SCORE = 5

LINDFIELD pattern. *Illustration from a Pairpoint Catalog*. DESIRABILITY SCORE = 5

MANSFIELD pattern shown on a #A-109 Bowl. *Illustration from a Pairpoint Catalog*. DESIRABILITY SCORE = 3

MAYFAIR pattern shown on a Clear # Unknown 17 Comport. DESIRABILITY SCORE = 3

MELROSE pattern. *Illustration from a Pairpoint Catalog*. DESIRABILITY SCORE = 3

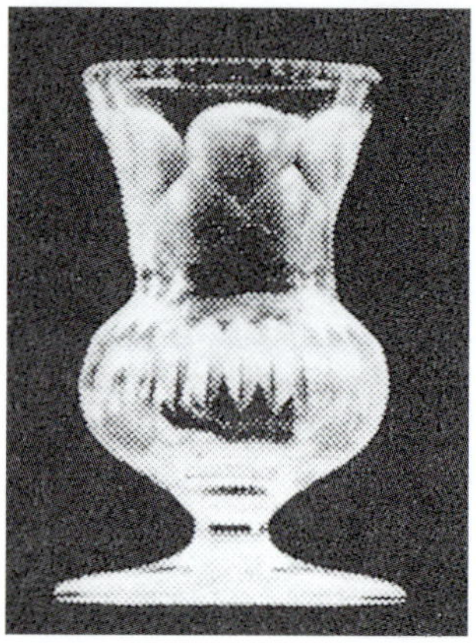

MITRE pattern shown on a #A-1077 Toothpick. *Illustration from a Pairpoint Catalog*. DESIRABILITY SCORE = 3

MONROE pattern shown on a Clear #1600 Candlestick. DESIRABILITY SCORE = 4

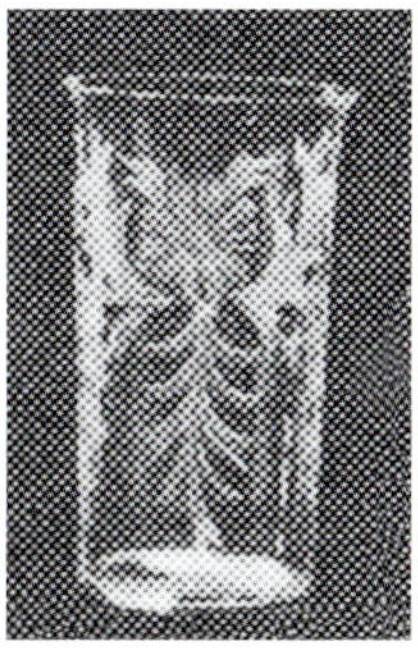

MORGAN pattern shown on a # Unknown 56 Tumbler. *Illustration from a Pairpoint Catalog.* DESIRABILITY SCORE = 3

MURILLO pattern shown on a Clear #336 Handled Plate. DESIRABILITY SCORE = 4

NOTTINGHAM pattern shown on a Clear #1635 Candlestick. DESIRABILITY SCORE = 4

NORFOLK pattern shown on a #A-194 Bowl. *Illustration from a Pairpoint Catalog.* DESIRABILITY SCORE = 4

No.33 pattern shown on a Clear #A-194 Bowl. DESIRABILITY SCORE = 2

No.136 pattern shown on a #6 Cologne. *Illustration from a Pairpoint Catalog.* DESIRABILITY SCORE = 2

No.129 pattern shown on a #8 Cologne. *Illustration from a Pairpoint Catalog.* DESIRABILITY SCORE = 3

No.151 pattern shown on a #458 Iced Tea Jug. *Illustration from a Pairpoint Catalog.* DESIRABILITY SCORE = 3

No.154 pattern shown on a Clear #A-1045 Vase. DESIRABILITY SCORE = 3

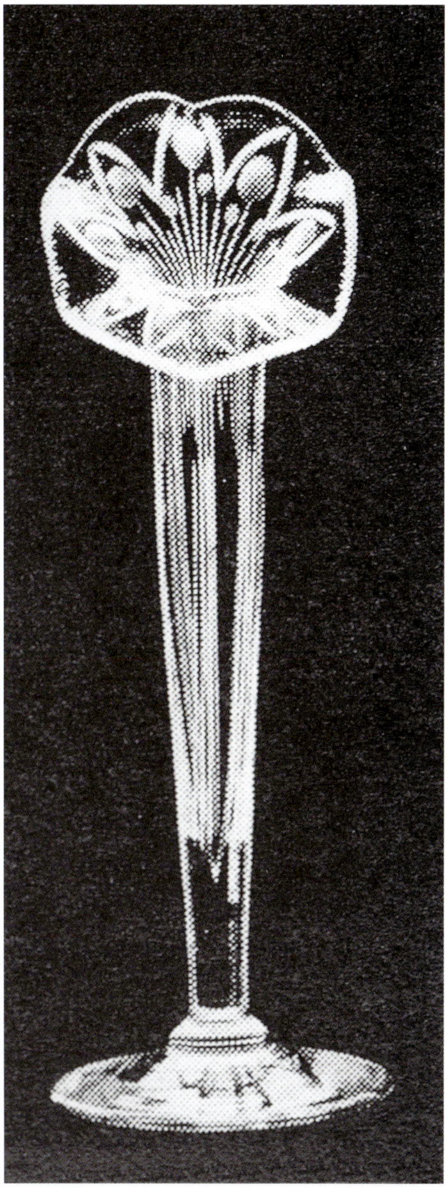

No.160 pattern shown on a #A-1046 Vase. *Illustration from a Pairpoint Catalog*. DESIRABILITY SCORE = 3

No.187 pattern shown on a #A-194 Bowl. *Illustration from a Pairpoint Catalog*. DESIRABILITY SCORE = 4

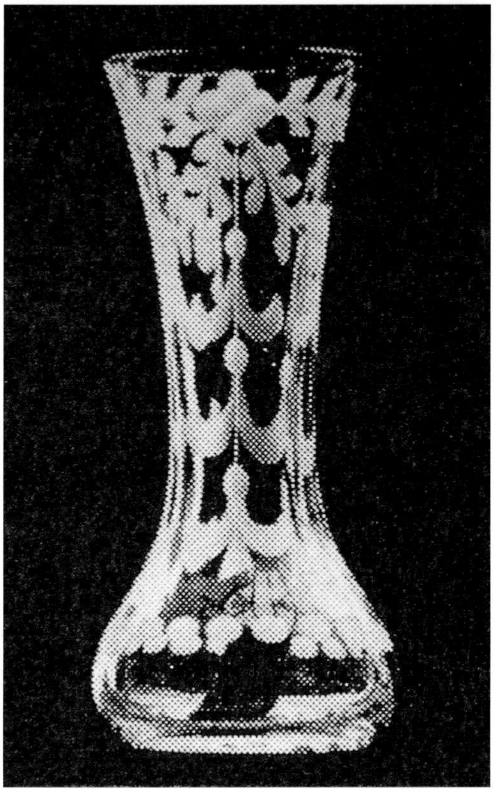

No.196 pattern shown on a 4.50" #A-1027 Vase. *Illustration from a Pairpoint Catalog*. DESIRABILITY SCORE = 3

No.192 pattern shown on a #1652 Jam Jar. *Illustration from a Pairpoint Catalog*. DESIRABILITY SCORE = 4

No.195 pattern shown on a #1653 Jam Jar. *Illustration from a Pairpoint Catalog*. DESIRABILITY SCORE = 4

No.245 pattern shown on a #150 Goblet. *Illustration from a Pairpoint Catalog*. DESIRABILITY SCORE = 3

No.246 pattern shown on a #150 Goblet. *Illustration from a Pairpoint Catalog.* DESIRABILITY SCORE = 2

No.258 pattern. *Illustration from a Pairpoint Catalog.* DESIRABILITY SCORE = 2

No.247 pattern shown on a #150 Goblet. *Illustration from a Pairpoint Catalog.* DESIRABILITY SCORE = 2

No.259 pattern. *Illustration from a Pairpoint Catalog.* DESIRABILITY SCORE = 2

No.6280 pattern shown on a #621 Decanter. *Illustration from a Pairpoint Catalog.* DESIRABILITY SCORE = 2

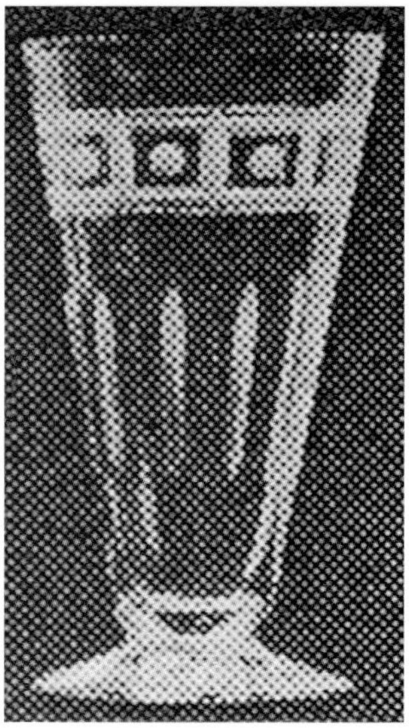

OPERA pattern shown on a # Unknown 55 Brandy & Soda Tumbler. *Illustration from a Pairpoint Catalog.* DESIRABILITY SCORE = 2

Below:
OLD COLONY pattern shown on a #156 Goblet. *Illustration from a Pairpoint Catalog.* DESIRABILITY SCORE = 4

OSIRIS pattern shown on a #A-1072 Vase. *Illustration from a Pairpoint Catalog.* DESIRABILITY SCORE = 5

PATCH DIAMOND pattern shown on a #642 Candlestick. *Illustration from a Pairpoint Catalog.* DESIRABILITY SCORE = 3

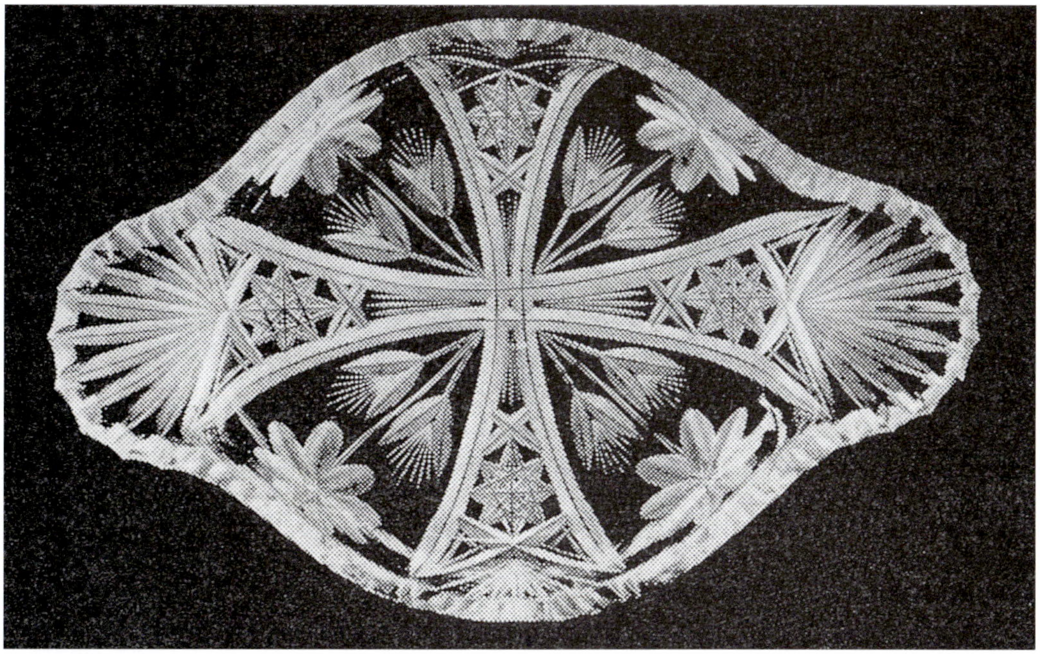

PLYMOUTH pattern shown on a #A-283 Nappy. We would describe this pattern as transitional with its origins in the Brilliant period. *Illustration from a Pairpoint Catalog.* DESIRABILITY SCORE = 5

POLAR BEAR pattern shown on a Clear #1159 Ice Pail. DESIRABILITY SCORE = 4

PORTSMOUTH pattern shown on a #A-194 Bowl and #1600 Candlesticks. *Illustration from a Pairpoint Catalog.* DESIRABILITY SCORE = 5

PRINCESS pattern shown on a #A-194 Bowl. *Illustration from a Pairpoint Catalog.* DESIRABILITY SCORE = 5

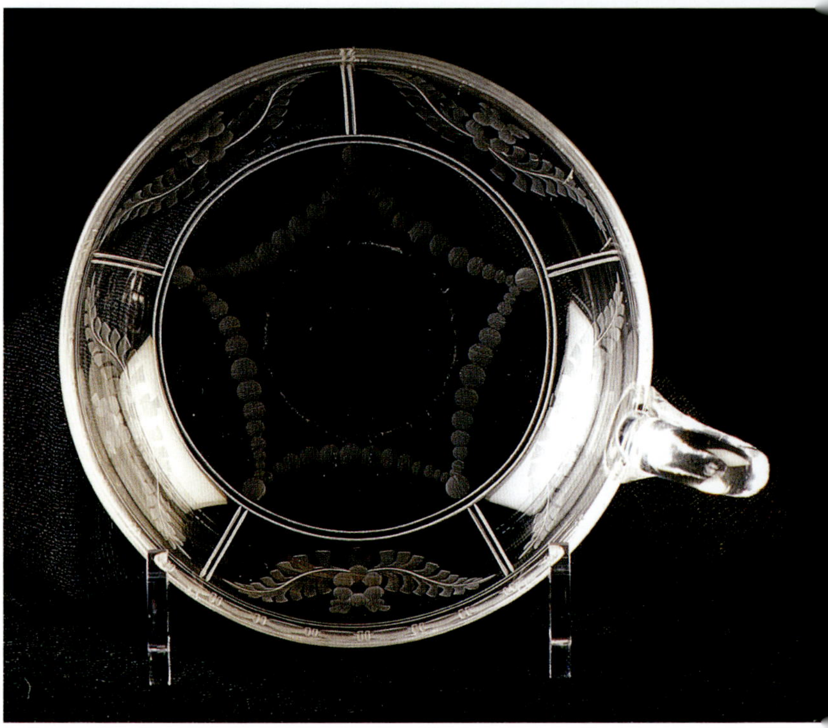

ROCKFORD pattern shown on a Clear # Unknown 69 Nappy. DESIRABILITY SCORE = 2

PUNTY & RAISED DIAMOND pattern shown on a #631 Decanter. *Illustration from a Pairpoint Catalog.* DESIRABILITY SCORE = 3

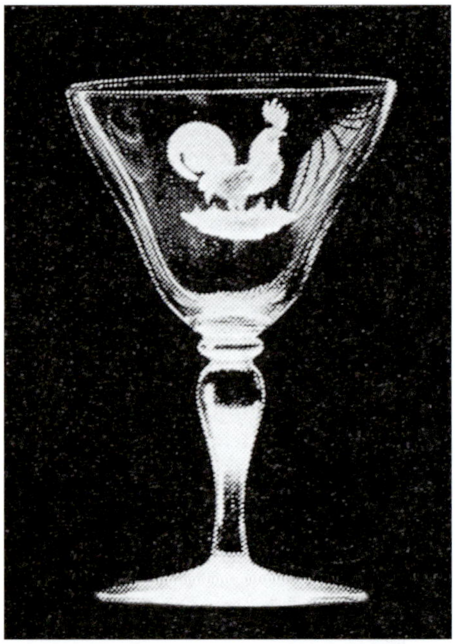

ROOSTER pattern shown on a #1072 Cocktail. *Illustration from a Pairpoint Catalog.* DESIRABILITY SCORE = 5

RICHMOND pattern. *Illustration from a Pairpoint Catalog.* DESIRABILITY SCORE = 5

ROYAL FERN pattern shown on a #A-194 Bowl. DESIRABILITY SCORE = 2

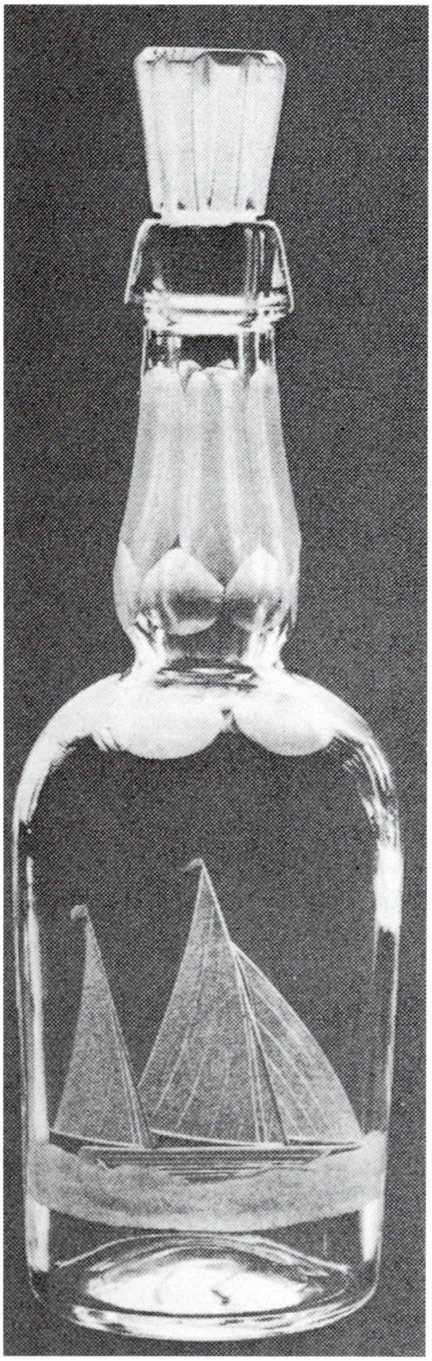

SCHOONER pattern shown on a #621 Decanter. *Illustration from a Pairpoint Catalog*. DESIRABILITY SCORE = 5

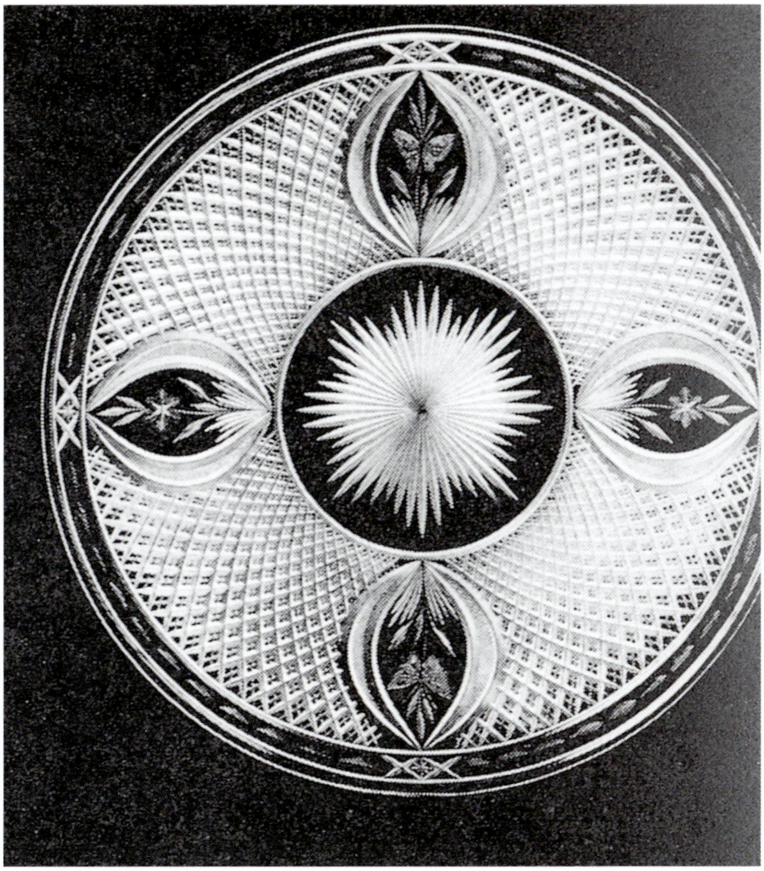

SIRIUS pattern. *Illustration from a Pairpoint Catalog*. DESIRABILITY SCORE = 5

SPANISH GALLEON pattern shown on a #1159 Ice Pail. *Illustration from a Pairpoint Catalog.* DESIRABILITY SCORE = 5

STRAWBERRY DIAMOND & FAN pattern shown on a 1/2 Pint Tumbler. *Illustration from a Pairpoint Catalog.* DESIRABILITY SCORE = 4

STAFFORDSHIRE pattern shown on a #A-194 Bowl. *Illustration from a Pairpoint Catalog.* DESIRABILITY SCORE = 5

STRAWBERRY pattern shown on a #1653 Jam Jar. *Illustration from a Pairpoint Catalog.* DESIRABILITY SCORE = 4

TASSEL pattern shown on a #5015 Goblet. *Illustration from a Pairpoint Catalog*. DESIRABILITY SCORE = 3

VICEROY pattern shown on a #2231 Crystalline Vase (see "Special Products" chapter). *Illustration from a Pairpoint Catalog*. DESIRABILITY SCORE = 2

TYRONE pattern shown on a Clear #A-228 Comport. DESIRABILITY SCORE = 3

VICTORIA pattern shown on a Clear #A-228 Comport. DESIRABILITY SCORE = 5

VISCARIA pattern shown on a Clear #1089 Sweet Pea Vase. DESIRABILITY SCORE = 3

WATERFORD pattern shown on a Clear #A-294 Comport. DESIRABILITY SCORE = 4

WELLINGTON pattern shown on a Clear #A-1062 Vase. DESIRABILITY SCORE = 4

WEXFORD pattern shown on the foot of an Amethyst #B-1811 Candlestick. DESIRABILITY SCORE = 4

WICKHAM pattern shown on a Green #A-294 Comport. DESIRABILITY SCORE = 5

WILTON pattern shown on a Clear # Unknown 45 Cornucopia Vase. DESIRABILITY SCORE = 4

WINDMILL pattern shown on a #C1543 Fine Arts Line Vase. *Illustration from a Pairpoint Catalog*. DESIRABILITY SCORE = 5

WREN pattern shown on a #B-1083 Vase. *Illustration from a Pairpoint Catalog*. DESIRABILITY SCORE = 2

UNKNOWN "B" pattern shown on a Green # Unknown 02 Bowl. DESIRABILITY SCORE = 3

UNKNOWN "A" pattern shown on a #150 Goblet. *Illustration from a Pairpoint Catalog*. DESIRABILITY SCORE = 2

UNKNOWN "C" pattern shown on a Clear #1159 Ice Pail. DESIRABILITY SCORE = 5

UNKNOWN "E" pattern shown on a Clear #A-194 Bowl. *Courtesy of Mrs. Marion E. Frost, Sr.* DESIRABILITY SCORE = 5

UNKNOWN "D" pattern shown on a Clear # Unknown 22 Comport. DESIRABILITY SCORE = 4

UNKNOWN "F" pattern shown on a Clear # Unknown 15 Candlestick. DESIRABILITY SCORE = 2

UNKNOWN "G" pattern shown on a Clear #A-1032 Vase. DESIRABILITY SCORE = 4

UNKNOWN "H" pattern shown on a Clear #1600 Candlestick. DESIRABILITY SCORE = 3

UNKNOWN "I" pattern shown on a Clear #A-228 Comport. DESIRABILITY SCORE = 4

UNKNOWN "K" pattern shown on a Clear #5000 Goblet with a square foot. DESIRABILITY SCORE = 4

UNKNOWN "J" pattern shown as two views on a "Colored Edge" Vase from the "Special Products" chapter. The only times we have seen this pattern have been on "Colored Edge and Trim" products. DESIRABILITY SCORE = 4

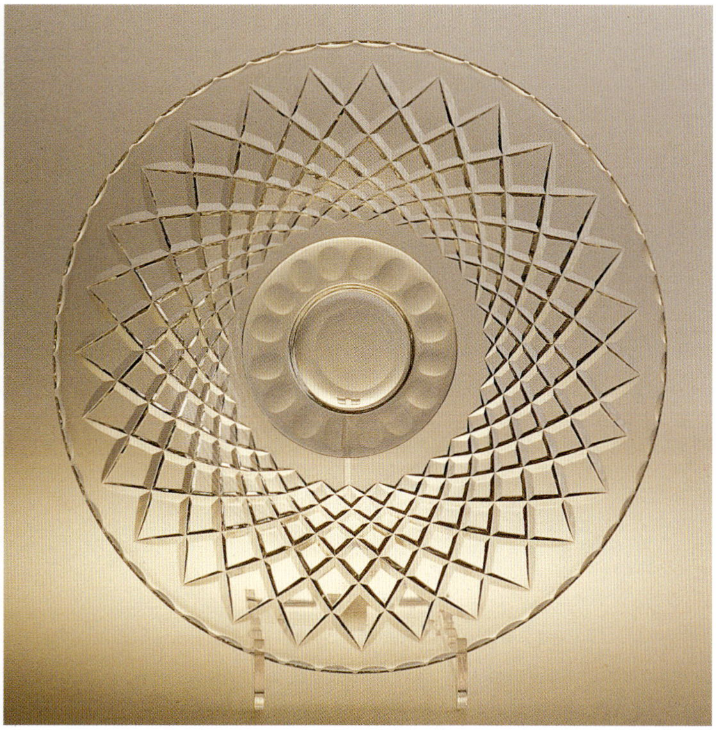

UNKNOWN "L" pattern shown on a Clear #A-194 Bowl. This pattern is most likely from the Gundersen period (1939-1952). *Courtesy of Craig and Christine Meraklis*. DESIRABILITY SCORE = 3

UNKNOWN "M" pattern shown on a # Unknown 83 Candelabrum. DESIRABILITY SCORE = 2

UNKNOWN "N" pattern shown on a #B-366 Comport that has a modified hollow foot intended to be merged with a silver-plated metal base and become an item from Pairpoint's Fine Arts Line. DESIRABILITY SCORE = 3

Chapter 4
Colors

Color Summary and Desirability Scores

(for chart on page 15)

	SCORE		SCORE
AMETHYST	4	FLAMBEAU	5
AURORIA (amber)	1	GREEN	3
BLACK AMETHYST (black)	5	GREEN-EMERALD	4
CANARIA (vaseline)	4	MARINA BLUE	4
CHRYSOPRAS	1	ROSARIA (cranberry)	5
CLEAR/COLORLESS	2	RUBY RED	4
COBALT BLUE	5		

General Comments About Colors

Before we get into the specific characteristics of each of the Pairpoint colors, it will be helpful to define two words that are used frequently when describing colors. Since we are automatically at a disadvantage when we try to *verbally* describe a characteristic that is normally *seen*, the accuracy of our choice of words becomes of paramount importance. A color *hue* is the relative position of the color on a color wheel. A color *shade* is the degree of brightness (lighter vs. darker) of any specific hue.

In an earlier section of this book (How to Use This Book), we made some general comments about the use of colors in determining the attribution of a piece of glass. While we steadfastly maintain that the reader will generally find color to be the least helpful element in identifying glass, it can be the most conclusive at times. In addition to the actual color, the maker's style or habit of utilizing colors in conjunction with other colors or clear glass within a single example can provide valuable clues for identification. For example, Morgantown made a centerpiece bowl (just like the Bristol Yellow Steuben bowl we described earlier in this book) that appears more identical to Pairpoint's Shape #A-194 than the Steuben bowl did. Morgantown's bowl was made in amethyst and had a clear glass foot. Pairpoint did not utilize clear feet on their colored bowls. This explained other anomalies that were easy to *overlook* if you wanted this bowl to be Pairpoint's; the glass did not *ring* properly and the foot diameter was disproportionately large.

Study colors as you meander through shows or view collections. Also study how the colors are used within a design and how the colors sound (don't forget our warning about ringing someone else's glass). By combining this knowledge with other tiny bits of knowledge gathered along the way, the path to more accurate attribution, or more often non-attribution, becomes much better marked.

AMETHYST- This color is a generic amethyst tending toward violet as opposed to purple. Over the years it has been our experience that when Amethyst pieces are found engraved, it is generally with one of the more formal and sophisticated patterns. The *Grape* pattern is probably the most likely pattern to find in Amethyst. *NOTE: When items of this color are tapped lightly, they generally will "ring" with a bell-tone quality and have good resonance. Also, when viewed under a black light, Amethyst does not fluoresce.*

An **AMETHYST** #B-960 Vase.

AURORIA (Amber)- Unlike some of the other glass companies of their time, Pairpoint utilized one color of amber. It was a rich, warm medium shade that leaned toward a reddish-golden hue. Depending upon the thickness and shape of the object being viewed, Auroria could appear lighter or darker from light transmission, but the hue remained constant. Although amber is generally considered one of the least desirable colors in glassware, Pairpoint's Auroria carries itself well in many of the shapes, especially those incorporating the clear bubble-ball connector. True to the color of natural amber which was popular in jewelry items, the use of Auroria was largely discontinued by the end of the Middle Period (1938). *NOTE: When items of this color are tapped lightly, they generally will "ring" with a slightly tinny bell-tone quality and will have good resonance. Also, when viewed under a black light, Auroria appears to fluoresce, but in a barely discernible way.*

An **AURORIA** Console set comprised of a #B-369 Bowl and (2) #B-1627 Candlesticks.

BLACK AMETHYST (Black)- This color appears black and, for all general discussion, it is. However, when held to an extremely intense light source (like the sun) and viewed through a thin cross-section area, a purple color will be observed. Many glass companies that made black glass actually made black amethyst. Pairpoint *only* made black amethyst; if the purple hue is not visible, it is not Pairpoint.

This is a relatively scarce color to find; when you do come across a piece made from Black Amethyst glass, it is very likely to find it with a sterling silver overlay decoration (perhaps 50% of the time). It is also occasionally found used in conjunction with Pairpoint's Flambeau color (see Flambeau), as well as clear/colorless. We have never seen black amethyst pieces decorated by engraving, but on page 23, of George Avila's book, *The Pairpoint Glass Story*, a photograph shows an engraved pattern on a black glass blank. Black Amethyst was not available beyond the Middle Period, and is a very desirable color to have. *NOTE: When items of this color are tapped lightly, they will "ring" flat and clunky and will resonate very poorly. Also, when viewed under a black light, Black Amethyst does not fluoresce.*

A **BLACK AMETHYST** #B-1007 Vase.

A **BLACK AMETHYST** #B-228 Comport with sterling silver overlay in a floral motif.

An example of **BLACK AMETHYST** merged with **CLEAR** on a #A-294 Comport.

CANARIA (Vaseline)- This color is more generically known as Vaseline, but in our opinion, does not display the bright garishness found on many of the more common pressed glass pieces found on the market today. When viewed along an edge looking *into* the piece as opposed to looking *through* the piece, the coloration changes to a beautiful fluorescing gray-green. To observe the effect of sunlight coming through a window onto a display of Canaria glass is to see a constantly changing display of yellow to green hues. Using uranium oxide as an ingredient in the batch formulation, this color was probably not made much past the early 1930s. When found engraved the most common patterns are *Grape* and *Osiris*. Even though Canaria is one of those colors that you either like or you don't, it is worth obtaining for your collection because it is relatively scarce. *NOTE: When items of this color are tapped lightly, they generally will "ring" with a somewhat tinny bell-tone quality and have very good resonance. Also, when viewed under a black light, Canaria will fluoresce a very bright yellowish-green.*

A **CANARIA** #B-959 Vase.

CHRYSOPRAS (Brown)- This color is elusive; in fact, we are not absolutely certain we have even seen it! Described by Shuman (1) as being *brown streaks* and by Padgett (2) as being *brown*, we opt for the latter description as being brown in color. We choose this option for a couple of reasons. First of all Pairpoint was not known for using mottled colors or streaks as a form of decoration; the use of solid colors was their traditional style. Secondly we have a vase in our collection, and have also viewed at glass shows, pieces of Pairpoint glass (unquestionably so) that are medium-dark brown in color with a leaning toward yellow on a color wheel.. There is no way the creative mind could say this color is just an amber variant; the color is unique unto itself.. Until we learn something to the contrary, we are showing this color under the name *Chrysopras* in the color plates.

We have also seen this color used by Pairpoint as accent trimming on various bowls, comports, and vases. It appears sometimes as an applied edge or as a stem connector in an assortment of shapes. When we have seen it used this way, it has usually been on a clear glass piece that is decorated with either the *Waterford* engraving pattern or an unnamed *floral design with trailing vines*. We think this color would be considered by most people to be unattractive. We would speculate that Pairpoint found Chrysopras to be unpopular, thus giving rise to the fact that it is probably the hardest color to find today. *NOTE: When items of this color are tapped lightly, they will "ring" with a somewhat tinny bell-tone quality and have very good resonance. Also, when viewed under a black light, Chrysopras does not fluoresce.*

A **CHRYSOPRAS** #A-1064 Vase.

CLEAR/COLORLESS- *Colorless* was the term used to describe the near-perfect glass produced by the Dorflinger Company in the 19th and early 20th centuries. So perfect and fine was their clarity, that once you have seen Dorflinger's glass, you can actually use clarity as a defining characteristic in a marginal attribution. In our humble opinion, we believe Pairpoint's clear glass approaches that of Dorflinger's with regard to its purity and clarity. Although most collectors prefer colored Pairpoint glass over the clear, probably half of all Pairpoint glass you will find today will be clear. Seldom found plain (unengraved), you will be more likely to find the greatest variety of engraving patterns on clear glass pieces. This is in spite of the fact that Pairpoint would decorate almost any color with almost any engraving pattern. *NOTE: When items of this color are tapped lightly, they generally will "ring" with an outstanding bell-tone quality and have excellent resonance. Also, when viewed under a black light, Clear/Colorless glass will yield very interesting, but confusing, results. Approximately 70% of our collection will fluoresce a medium intensity frosty bluish-white, but the remaining 30%, which from their style indicates earlier production items (i.e.. Jugs, Venetti Design, etc.), will fluoresce a low intensity yellow-green. Obviously this inconsistency is the result of there being two different glass batch formulations. In George Avila's book,* The Pairpoint Glass Story*, page 205, he references glass fragments, which "show up as lemon yellow when given the black light test" being dug-up from the factory ruins which date to the time of the New Bedford Glass Works, the 1860s. According to Mr. Avila, this glass works was staffed by workers that had previously been involved in the making of Sandwich glass and more than likely had brought their clear glass formulations with them to New Bedford. It is our speculation that this old Sandwich formulation was utilized by Mt. Washington Glass and subsequently Pairpoint as their clear glass recipe. We also speculate that at some point in time, perhaps the mid-1920s, the clear glass formula was changed to that which produces the frosty bluish-white fluorescence when viewed under a black light. It appears to us that none of the Clear/Colorless Pairpoint pieces in our collection, that we believe to be of a later production period, fluoresce as "lemon yellow".*

A **CLEAR/COLORLESS** #B-1485 Vase.

COBALT BLUE- Like amethyst, Cobalt Blue as made by Pairpoint can best be described as generic. Cobalt is the darkest of the *blues* and is probably the most desirable of all the colors. A piece of glass in Cobalt will almost always command a higher price than its counterpart in another color. For this reason Cobalt pieces do not remain on the market for very long thus leaving the impression that they are scarce. On the contrary there are other colors that are considerably more scarce but their lower popularity keeps them available for a longer time, thereby making them seem more plentiful.

In addition to making articles completely from Cobalt Blue glass, Pairpoint incorporated this color, more than any other color, in the production of many of their special product lines and decorating treatments. In addition to products such as *Cobalt Swirl* and Carbone's *Pin Wheel* design, Cobalt was used as an accent on clear glass and with silver plated wares (EPNS) as feet and stems. The use of Cobalt glass as an overlay on Pairpoint's exquisite *cut-to-clear* pieces is particularly striking and noteworthy. (See the Special Products section for examples of the further use of Cobalt glass.) *NOTE: When items of this color are tapped lightly, they generally will "ring" with a bell-tone quality and have excellent resonance. Also, when viewed under a black light, Cobalt Blue does not fluoresce.*

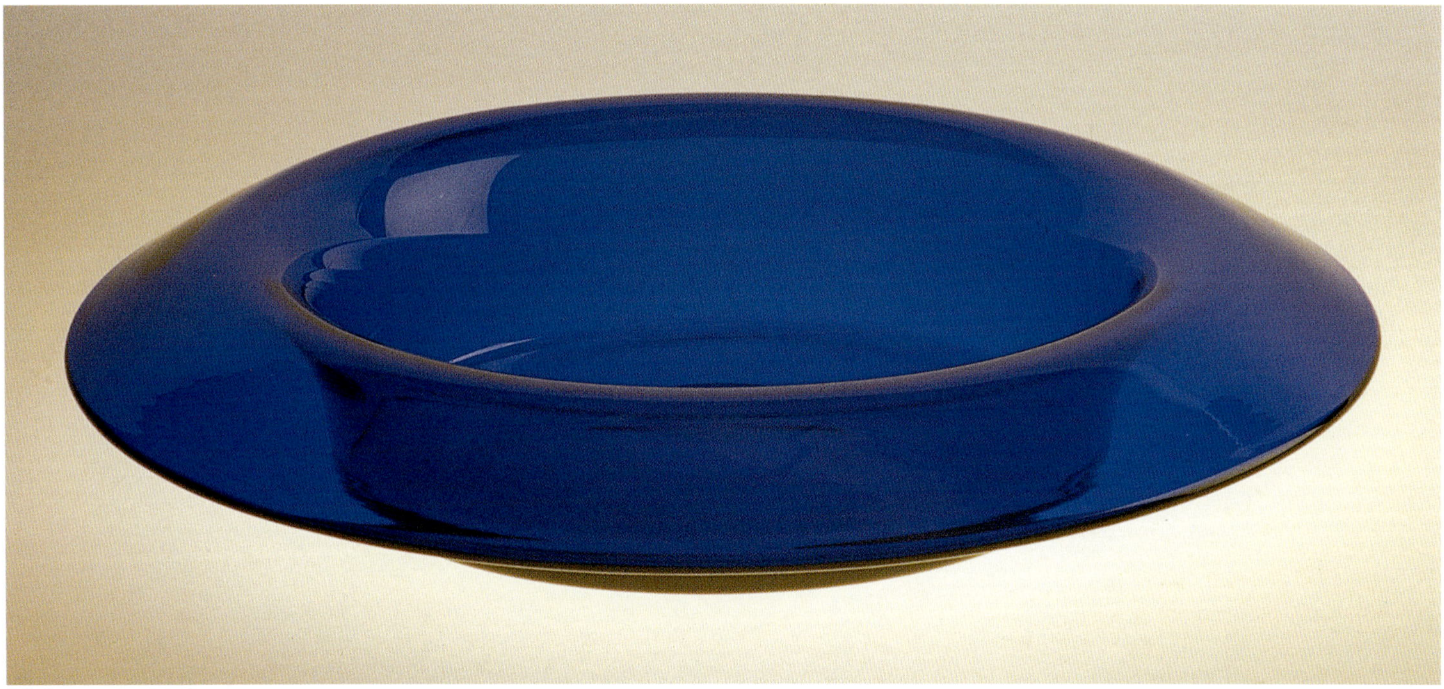

A **COBALT BLUE** #A-106 Centerpiece Bowl.

FLAMBEAU- This color is best described as Tomato Red/Orange or perhaps Chinese Red and is always *uniformly* opaque. Hues may vary from a pale orange-red to a more vivid red-orange from batch to batch but will always be uniform and homogeneous within a piece. Other makers of glass duplicated this color very closely, but you can often detect slight transparencies and streaking of color within the glass as if the glass didn't get mixed very well. It would be a sound idea to not rely on the existence of this color to attribute the piece to Pairpoint. Instead rely on the shapes.

This glass was very difficult to work and was produced for only a couple years during the early to middle 1920s. We have never seen Flambeau decorated by engraving, but in approximately 65% of the examples we have seen, the pieces have been decorated with a sterling silver overlay pattern. Although we are certain that some items would have been made entirely of Flambeau glass, every example we own or have seen in more than ten years has been a combination of Flambeau and Black Amethyst. *NOTE: When items of this color are tapped lightly, they will "ring" with a dull, flat sound and have mediocre resonance. Also, when viewed under a black light, Flambeau does not fluoresce.*

A **FLAMBEAU & BLACK AMETHYST** #B-366 Comport.

NOTE: In the marketplace you will regularly come upon stemware (usually cocktails) that have red-orange bowls and black stems/feet. These pieces are identical in almost every way to what Pairpoint would have produced. Upon close observation, 99.9% of the time, you will observe a very thin clear glass overlay applied to the piece. Pairpoint never applied a clear overlay to Flambeau; in all likelihood the examples with the overlay are of Czechoslovakian origin. Once you have seen Flambeau and the ever-so-slight *dullness* of the surface, you will be able to differentiate Pairpoint's product from the others.

A Cocktail glass that is easily mistaken for Pairpoint, but is believed to be Czeckoslovakian in origin. A clear overlay is the tell-tale feature. Pairpoint did not overlay their Flambeau color.

A detail view showing the clear overlay in the area where the stem meets the bowl. The overlay is very thin, but it does impart a high gloss sparkling appearance that is not evident with Pairpoint's Flambeau.

GREEN- This was a popular color used by everyone during the 1920s and 1930s, but fortunately can not be described in generic terms. There were so many hues and shades of green used that attribution can actually be made, by color, with some degree of accuracy. If there is any glass color more worthy of close study by the collector to aid in identification, we don't know what it would be. Pairpoint used a green hue that tended toward the yellow side of the color wheel....a *grass* green more than an *emerald* green. Some people have said and written that Pairpoint greens came in many hues, but we don't agree with that assertion. The batch formulation process was so accurate and well-controlled that the likelihood of there being various hues produced would have been remote. What we have noticed while handling hundreds of pieces in green is that the green color will change its shade depending upon the thickness and shape of the piece being viewed. These changes seem to be more related to intensity of color as you view the thick stem or the thin bowl component of a piece. Except for two variations that are described below, we have never seen Pairpoint's Green to be anything but a "yellow" green.

The two exceptions to what we have described above are what we believe to be special products made for perhaps a retail customer that wanted exclusivity in their product line. It is known that Pairpoint was very willing to grant exclusivity of engraving patterns to notable customers such as Tiffany's of New York. It should not be ruled-out that the same could have occurred with regard to colors.

A "standard" **GREEN** #B-1065 Bowl.

EXCEPTION 1. We have seen, and own, several examples of conventional shapes that are made from a hue of green glass that would appear more central on the color wheel....less yellow but not quite into blue. Every example but one that we have seen in this color variant has also been engraved with a floral pattern (Unknown "B") seemingly unique to these pieces but not identified as Pairpoint in any reference source.

An example of the "variant" hue of **GREEN** shown on a # Unknown 02 Bowl engraved in the Unknown "B" pattern.

EXCEPTION 2. In ten years we have seen five examples of Pairpoint shapes made from a dark shade of emerald green. In each case but two, both of which are in our collection, the pieces have been decorated with a sterling silver overlay design.

Green glass in general falls low on the list of desirable colors; this applies to Pairpoint glass as well. However, green was very popular during the Middle Period, and as a result many of Pairpoint's finest engraving patterns will be found on green blanks. The benefit to the collector over the past decade has been to find high quality pieces in green for rather moderate prices. But, we have noticed more recently a rapid upward trend in the pricing of Pairpoint green as quality examples of Pairpoint in any color are becoming increasingly scarce. Also a recognition by the public of Pairpoint's quality makes color preference less of a factor in the buying process. *NOTE: When items of this color are tapped lightly, they generally will "ring" with a bell-tone quality and have very good to excellent resonance. The emerald green will "ring" with a dull sound and resonate poorly. Also, when viewed under a black light, all hues of green will fluoresce a bright green. However, the emerald green will fluoresce to a lesser degree.*

An **EMERALD GREEN** #B-369 Bowl. This color is not seen very often.

MARINA BLUE- This is a difficult color to find in the earlier Pairpoint pieces; most examples found today probably date from the later Gundersen Period (1939-1952). Being a light shade of blue, leaning toward the gray tones, Marina Blue pieces are especially lovely when utilizing Pairpoint's well-known bubble ball connector in the stem or base. Marina Blue pieces are almost never seen with an engraved pattern; We have seen only one or two examples within the last ten years or so. It would be extremely difficult, if not impossible, to build a collection around this color; there just isn't very much of it. *NOTE: When items of this color are tapped lightly, they will "ring" with something less than a bell-tone quality and have a moderate resonance. Earlier pieces seem to "ring" better than later examples. Also, when viewed under a black light, Marina Blue will fluoresce a low intensity yellowish-green..*

ROSARIA- This was Pairpoint's version of Cranberry and was probably more prevalent in the latter part of the Middle Period and forward into the Gundersen era. Rosaria is not a common color to find made into entire pieces, although it certainly was. It is more common to find it as an overlay color on *cut-to-clear* pieces and, in the Gundersen Period, as accent ribbing or edging on clear pieces. When examples of Pairpoint glass are found made entirely of Rosaria glass, the blanks are generally found to have been formed utilizing a diamond or waffle optic pattern within the glass. This is essentially the limit of decoration on Rosaria pieces; we have only seen two examples with an engraving pattern applied. Rosaria is a very desirable color to find, and when you do, expect to pay an above average price. *NOTE: When items of this color are tapped lightly, they will "ring" with a wonderful bell-tone quality and have an excellent resonance. Also, when viewed under a black light, Rosaria will fluoresce a very low level yellow-green.*

A **MARINA BLUE** #B-1083 Vase.

A **ROSARIA** #B-366 Comport.

RUBY RED- The use of Ruby as a glass color goes back to the 1920s for Pairpoint, but reached the height of popularity during the later Gundersen Period (1939-1952). It is often difficult to determine when a piece of Ruby glass was manufactured since Gundersen carried many of the original Pairpoint shapes forward. And since we have never seen Ruby glass engraved, we can't use the existence of an early pattern to date an example. Therefore, the only way we can attempt to describe how to date a piece of Ruby glass is to rely on some basic characteristics. Earlier Ruby pieces generally utilized the famous bubble ball connector within their design; vases were a common shape to be made from Ruby glass. Earlier pieces would be more likely to use Ruby for the foot as well as the upper body of the piece. Recognizing the *older* style of a blank shape would be useful as an indicator of age. Later Gundersen pieces were becoming more contemporary. The use of a clear glass *swirl* connector or *swirl* base came about during the Gundersen Period. It was also characteristic of the Gundersen era to make the upper body of a shape from Ruby glass while the stem *and* foot would be made from clear glass. Although known earlier, Cornucopia vases became popular during the Gundersen years, and most examples found in Ruby probably date from that period.

Dating Ruby glass is difficult, because certainty is almost unachievable. In our opinion, the overriding strategy of the collector should be to try and acquire quality examples of Pairpoint glass whenever possible. The glass made during the Gundersen Period is of high quality and is available at prices lower than the quality should demand. It's just a matter of time before the market will take notice and prices will climb. *NOTE: When an item of this color is tapped lightly, it will "ring" with a flat and clunky sound and have mediocre to poor resonance. Also, when viewed under a black light, Ruby Red does not fluoresce.*

A **RUBY RED** #B-1485 Vase.

Chapter 5

Special Products

When valuing any item from the Special Products section, DO NOT USE the composite scoring method that we recommend for valuing the general product line (page 15).

Pairpoint products that fall outside of the product classification that we would refer to as *general inventory* are presented here. These products are unique in that they incorporate a variety of features that in combination do not appear in the regularly produced product line. Although they may utilize specific features used within the general line, the predominant theme will render the product line unique or *Special*.

As you proceed through each of the Special Product categories, you may readily notice those characteristics that are shared with the general product line. Some special products will use the conventional shapes but have modified features within the manufactured blank, such as color swirling. Other products will have unique shapes but utilize a commonly produced engraving pattern. Still other special products will be unique in all respects except color; Pairpoint never varied their colors.

Unlike Pairpoint's general product line, which is best attributed by following the step-by-step technique preached and repreached throughout this book, Special Products are *discovered* by recognizing the combination of features that yield a certain look. Once you become familiar with that look, by studying each of the product lines that follow, you will probably find that the Special Products are easier to identify than the general line items. Once you recognize the combination of features, the recognition of shapes becomes virtually (but not totally) unnecessary. For these, shapes should probably be ignored as the primary attribution factor. We have found many special product line items that, if not for the combination of features declaring themselves as Pairpoint, we would have classified as "very nice but maker unknown."

The Special Product categories that follow are organized alphabetically according to their official names, if applicable, or by their key features. Some of the better documented product lines will have photographs as well as catalog renderings, while others will only have photographs taken of specific examples we have found. In neither case should you consider what is shown to be the totality of the product line.

When pricing is shown, it will represent our estimate of what that specific piece would yield at a better glass show. The value of any special product item that is not shown within the relative categories would be determined by comparing the merits of the piece to those shown; in other words, by a judgment call.

Carbone Glass Company

Information relating to the product line allegedly produced for the Carbone Company, under their label, is extremely vague and elusive; some dealers will deny any collaboration at all. Through conversations with two or three knowledgeable dealers and editorial reference (*Pairpoint Glass* by Leonard Padgett, Page 192), all we can discern is that in addition to other products, clear crystal items with a spiral optic and reverse spiral cobalt blue pinwheel design were produced for Carbone sometime during the late Gundersen (1951-1952) and early post-Gundersen (1952-1957) eras. Our friends and advisors for this book, Charles and Barbara Coulter, found a large cache of Carbone labels and correspondence when they walked the ruins of the abandoned factory many years ago. To us, the existence of a relationship between the Pairpoint organization and Carbone is well documented and absolutely indisputable.

Although the time period for the Carbone product line is beyond that which is primarily covered by this book, these color and optical effects were incorporated within the same shapes as those produced during the Middle Period. Due to the similarities involved, we felt to exclude this product line because of the era of production would only lead to confusion and incorrect time conclusions on the part of the collector. In addition to the use of the *old* shapes, these items will be found with polished pontils and will exhibit very good workmanship. You will occasionally find a Carbone item that reflects the more contemporary fashion of the 1950s, so your correct attribution may be hesitant because of the absence of the traditional Pairpoint classic look.

These pieces are *very* scarce and should be acquired whenever possible. Look first for the traditional Pairpoint shape, but if you find an item of a newer, less recognizable style, the distinctive optic spiraling with the reverse blue pinwheel effect should remove any doubts you have about origin.

A Carbone Bowl, Shape #A-194, 12" d. $500.

A Carbone Bowl, Shape #A-106, 13" d. $475.

A Carbone Covered Candy Dish, 7.50" overall height x 7.50" diameter. $650.

Cased Glass Cut-to-Clear

This is one of those design effects that is staggeringly beautiful when done properly. In simple terms the process involves layering two colors of glass (clear is almost always one of the colors) during the manufacture of the blank. When completed the blank is sent to the cutting/engraving department where a design is cut through the color layer thus exposing the clear layer. In actuality the process was not that simple. It required a high level of precision in the layering of the colors, the shaping of the blank, and ultimately the cutting or engraving.

Attribution is relatively straight forward as cut-to-clear pieces utilized the same standard shapes and decorating patterns that were used for normal production items; the blanks would be of the thicker variety for obvious reasons. In most cases the colored layer of glass was Cobalt Blue or Rosaria. Cut-to-clear pieces are very scarce and command a premium price whenever they are offered for sale; even though a dealer may not know the Pairpoint origin of a specific piece, the quality speaks boldly: "I am wonderful...price me high!"

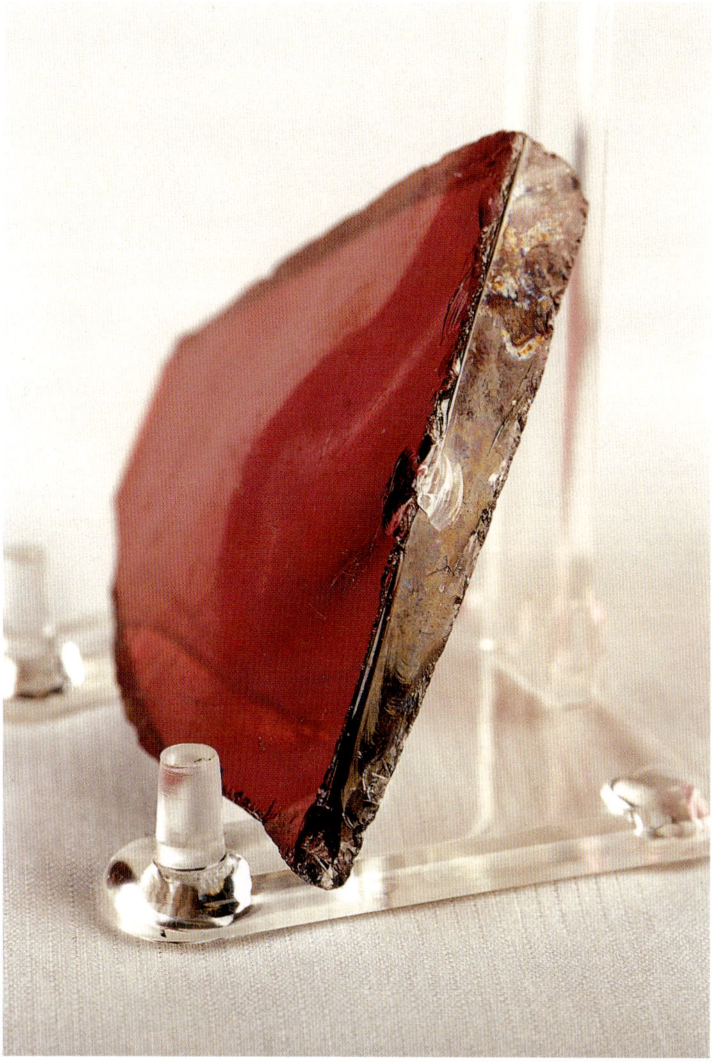

A glass shard, dug from the abandoned Pairpoint factory site by Charles Coulter, that shows the Rosaria color layered over clear glass. A design would have then been cut or engraved into and through the Rosaria layer, exposing the clear base. *Courtesy of Charles and Barbara Coulter.*

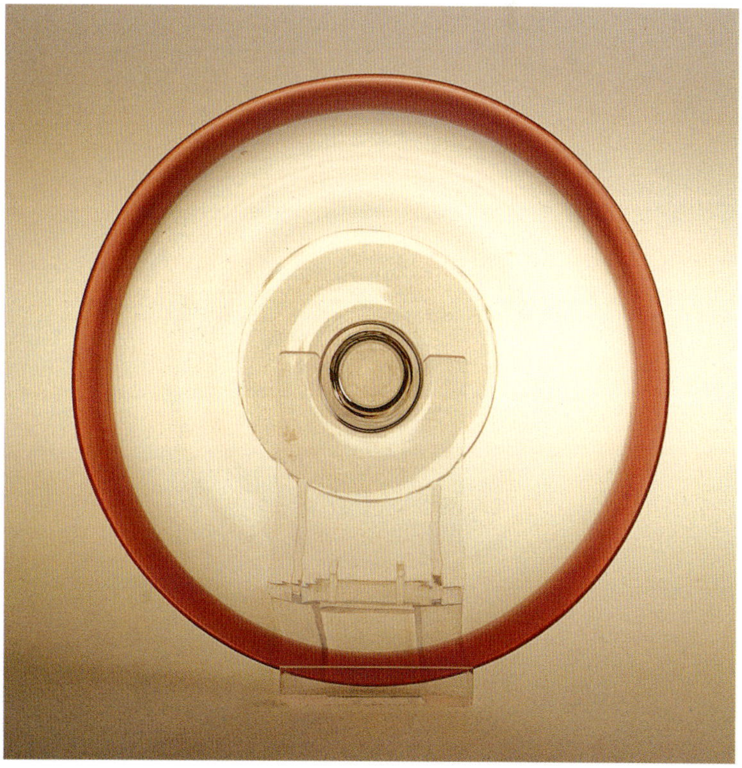

A top view of a #A-228 Comport showing the Rosaria glass band layered over the Clear bowl edge. This unfinished piece would most likely have been engraved in the Darlington pattern had something not interrupted the production process.

An example of a # Unknown 19 Comport engraved in the Darlington pattern. $850. (The price shown is lower than that which our pricing formula for cut-to-clear glass would dictate because the cased glass effect is limited to a narrow edge banding.)

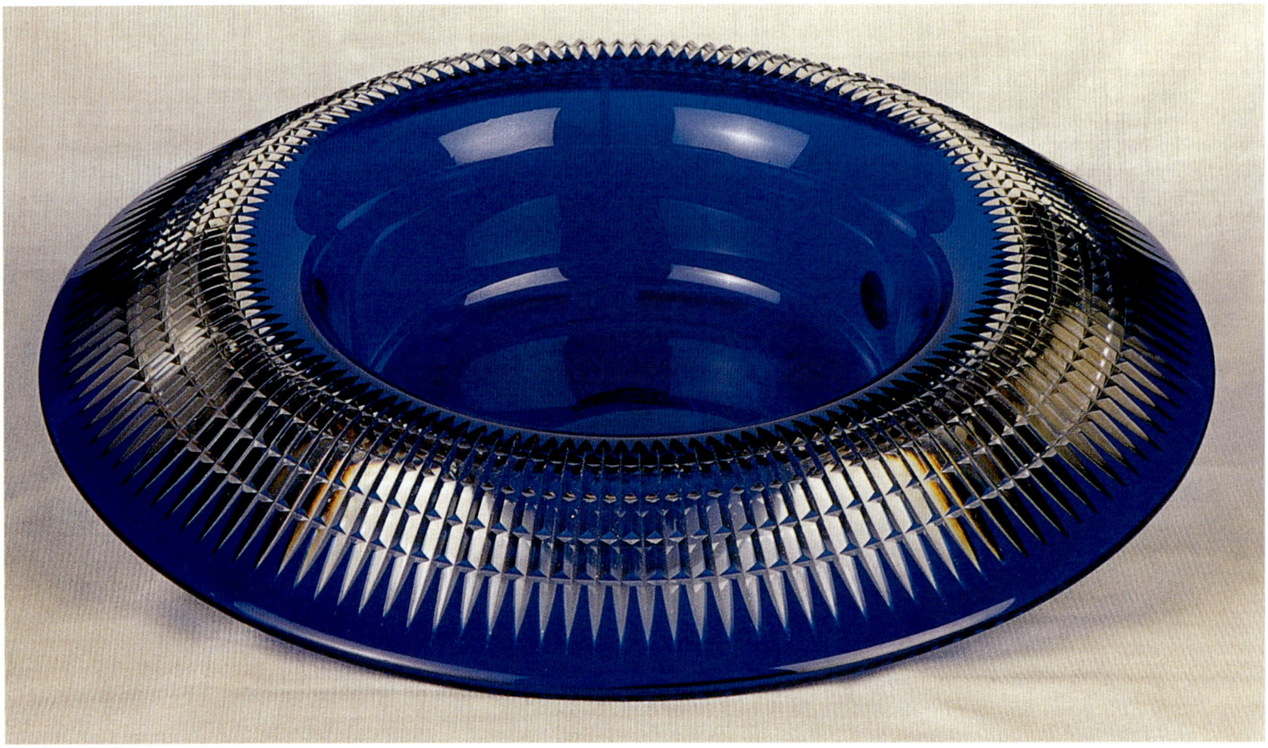

A #A-106 Centerpiece Bowl, Cobalt Blue cut-to-clear. $760.

A #B-1485 Vase, Rosaria cut-to-clear in the Lincoln pattern. $1,430.

Colored Edge and Trim

During the last few years, we have seen an ever-increasing presence of clear glass items, unquestionably of Pairpoint origin, that are trimmed in Cobalt Blue, Amethyst, or Chrysopras (brown). The colored trim usually exists as narrow edge bands, handles, stem connectors, and/or spiral *barber pole-style* threading on stems. Every example we have seen, except for the vase photographed below, has been engraved with the Waterford pattern or the as yet unnamed floral pattern (see Unknown "J") also shown below. The blanks upon which this colored trim appears are not perfectly consistent with those of the Middle Period; the styles suggest that this line of products could have been made during a later period, such as the late 1940s or early 1950s, but the quality of workmanship and the use of the color Chrysopras suggests that the line was made during the 1920s or 1930s. To date we have not found any authoritative reference to pinpoint a manufacturing period. We are *in the dark* on this one; can anyone out there help?

An example of a Vase having a Chrysopras top edge, bottom edge, and ball connector. The absence of an engraved design is unusual. 9.50" h. $150.

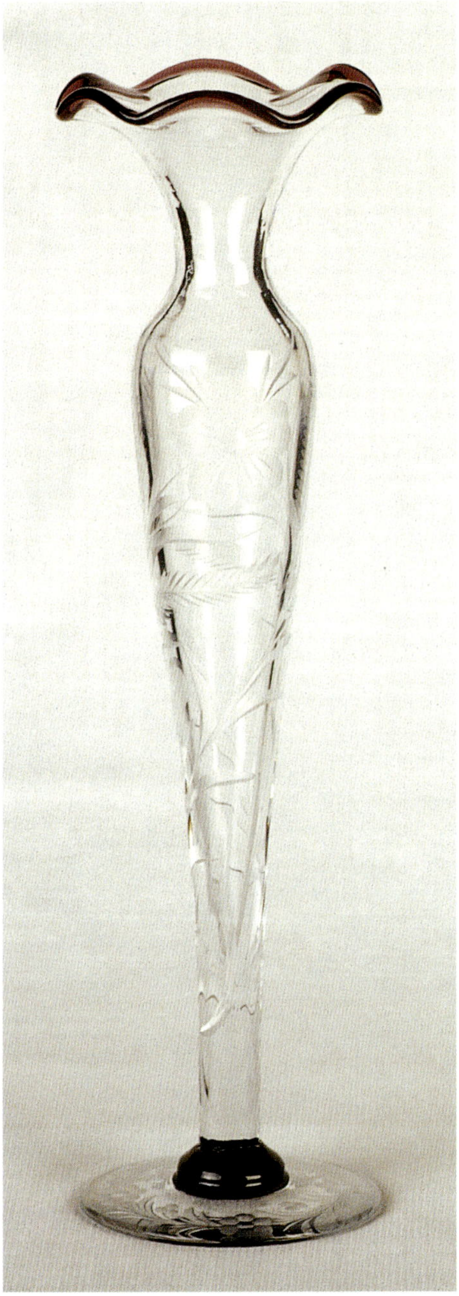

An example of a Bud Vase having an Amethyst top edge, bottom edge, and connecting wafer. This vase is engraved in the floral pattern # UNKNOWN "J", which we have found only on these "Colored Edge and Trim" pieces. 11.50" h. $300.

Color Twist Glass, Red or Blue

This technique was used on a limited number of standard inventory shapes made during the Middle Period, as well as on slightly modified shapes that were created just for this product line. Ruby Red and Cobalt Blue were the only colors used to create this very unique visual effect. The process involved required the highest level of skill and rendered a product so beautiful that no further decoration was required.

This product line was made during the 1920s, and is very difficult to find today. There probably exists some *sleepers* out there, but if you want to own one of these gems, be prepared to pay a *king's ransom* to a quality glass dealer who will be sorry to see it go.

A Color Twist #3015 Comport, 8" d x 4.625" h. *Illustration from a Pairpoint Catalog.* $650.

A Color Twist #3019 Bowl, (12" d), 14" d, 16" d. *Illustration from a Pairpoint Catalog.* $850.

A Color Twist Comport #3016, 8" d x 4.625" h. *Illustration from a Pairpoint Catalog.* $650.

A Color Twist #B-3020 Bowl, 12" d. *Illustration from a Pairpoint Catalog.* $950.

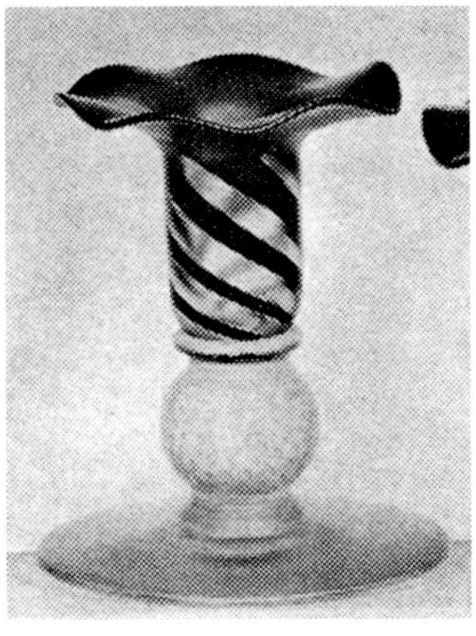

A Color Twist #B-3021 Candlestick, 5" h. *Illustration from a Pairpoint Catalog.* $300.

A Color Twist #B-3024 Candlestick, Ruby, 5" h. $300.

A wonderful example of a Copper Comport with Pewter Trim, #X1422, 6.5" d x 6.00" h. The comport has a ribbed bowl and foot and a molded pewter hexagonal stem. $200.

Copper Ware with Pewter Trim

During the late 1920s and early 1930s, Pairpoint was still actively engaged in the manufacturing of decorative items made from various metals, the most common of which were silver-plated wares. Among the most elusive of Pairpoint's metal products, and equal in scarcity to their Enamel Ware, is their line of Copper Ware with Pewter Trim. The two metals were artistically merged to create approximately twenty very elegant and beautifully executed forms that are striking to the eye. Occasionally an item from this line will be found with one surface (ie. the inside of a bowl) silver-plated.

All Copper Ware with Pewter Trim items are signed in the normal way with the letter "X" preceding the item number. You will probably be able to acquire an example for a modest sum, far below what its quality and scarcity should command.

Crystalline Glass

This product line was the manifestation of Pairpoint's belief that the basic material from which an object was made, the glass itself, could provide the final decorative appeal. Without the use of colors, paints, or engraving, the perfection and absolute clarity of the glass medium, formed into pleasing complimentary shapes, could be the ultimate and final form of decoration. Long-touted as producing the finest crystal glass anywhere, the C. Dorflinger & Co. rarely capitalized on the stand-alone beauty of their glass. Instead, their products were usually cut, engraved, or decorated in some other way. We are speculating that the Crystalline Glass product line could have been Pairpoint's competitive response to Dorflinger. "See...our glass is just as perfect as yours, and we aren't afraid to let the world see it!"

Crystalline Glass is striking in its simplicity, but did not become a big item for Pairpoint until later years. The shapes created were unique to this line, but definitely retained the *flavor* of Pairpoint's general product line. Upon occasion Crystalline Glass will be found engraved. Recognition of these items should not be too difficult.

A Crystalline #2227 Bowl with a square-cut base, 14" d x 4" h. *Illustration from a Pairpoint Catalog*. $300.

A Crystalline #2228 Bowl with a hollow foot. *Illustration from a Pairpoint Catalog*. $250.

A Crystalline #2230 Bowl with a hollow foot, 10" d x 3.25" h. *Illustration from a Pairpoint Catalog*. $250.

A Crystalline #2229 Bowl with a hollow foot. *Illustration from a Pairpoint Catalog*. $250.

A Crystalline #2231 Handled and Footed Vase with a square-cut base, engraved in the Viceroy pattern, 11.50" h. *Illustration from a Pairpoint Catalog*. $500.

A Crystalline #2232 Handled and Footed Vase with a square-cut base, 11.50" h. *Illustration from a Pairpoint Catalog.* $400.

A Crystalline Handled and Footed Vase with a square-cut base. *Illustration from a Pairpoint Catalog.* $400.

EPNS with Cobalt Blue

EPNS is the acronym for **E**lectro-**P**lated **N**ickel **S**ilver and was a style of silver plating used on a regular basis by Pairpoint. For our descriptive purposes here, and to help define this product line, it signifies a formed metal shape that has been combined with Cobalt Blue glass to create a very lovely and well-crafted decorative item. In every example we have seen, the upper body of a standard inventory shape is metal, and the foot is made of blue glass. Often the famous Pairpoint bubble ball is present with the metal portion joining at the top of the ball. The shape, sizing, and proportion of the metal work is reasonably true to that of its glass counterparts. However, unlike most of its all-glass siblings, the Cobalt Blue foot is of a flat-domed configuration, with the height of the *dome* being approximately 1/2" to 5/8". We have seen five or six examples of this product line during the last ten years, so we would have to represent this line to be relatively scarce. Unfortunately, when you do find an example, there is a high probability that the electro-plating will be flaking-off in spots; A reputable silversmith should be able to rectify this problem quite easily. (We refer you to the *Support Services* chapter near the end of the book for our recommendation.) Watch your costs, however. The price you will probably pay for an EPNS w/Cobalt piece will be higher than the same shape in all-glass unengraved. When added to your purchase price, the cost to strip and replate the metalwork could drive your total cost much higher than you might expect to pay for a perfect specimen, if you can find one.

It is easy to recognize items from this product line; they will almost always be of a conventional shape. To erase any doubt, look at an unobtrusive area of the metalwork for the Pairpoint signature (P within a diamond), the item number, and the inscription "E.P.N.S. - W.M.MOUNTS". If our memory has not totally abandoned us, most, if not all, of the examples we have encountered have utilized a flat-domed (sometimes referred to as *hollow*) foot. When this is the case, due to the method of holding the glass portion during manufacturing, you should not expect to find a pontil mark.

An example of a Pairpoint Comport having an E.P.N.S. bowl and stem, a clear bubble ball connector, and a flat-domed foot in Cobalt Blue. This is probably the most common form found, although we have seen pedestal bowls and vases from time to time. Every example of this product line we have seen has had the same impressed signature placed inconspicuously on the metal portion. Due to the method of working the glass, you will find no pontil mark. 8" d x 6" h. $300.

Enamel Ware

This little-known product line was probably produced sometime during the third and fourth decades of the twentieth century, and little is known about it. The basic form of each item is fabricated from a very heavy gauge of solid hammered copper and exhibits the styles of the glass decorative items from the period. A colored enamel solution, or coating, was applied to one of the interior surfaces, and the piece was then fired in an oven to cause the enamel to melt and bond to the base copper. The translucence of the thin enamel layer allows light to penetrate to the hammered copper undersurface and reflect at different angles simultaneously...all in all, a very pleasant effect. When found today the copper will probably be oxidized to a dark reddish-brown color and should be left that way. It would take a very long time for this patina to return to a polished copper surface.

Pairpoint signed these pieces by stamping their logo and product number into the copper surface in some obscure area; the product number will always be preceded by the letter "G". For those who can't identify Enamel Ware by any of the obvious appearance characteristics, the existence of the "G" is the giveaway.

These items are very scarce and should be purchased whenever possible. In over ten years of collecting, we have only seen two examples, and we purchased them both. In spite of the scarcity and the high quality of manufacture, you can expect to find pricing to be rather low. We think this has more to do with a general lack of knowledge than it has to do with quality issues.

A #G1460 Enamel Ware Comport of hammered copper with green glass enameling on the interior of the bowl, 6" d x 2.75" h. $250.

A #G5597 Enamel Ware Bowl of hammered copper with orange enameling on the interior of the bowl, 7" d x 4.75" h. $300.

A detail view showing the style of signature used by Pairpoint on their Enamel Ware products. Also, the detail provides a good view of the surface texture caused by the hammering of the copper into shape.

Fine Arts Line

The product line definitely had its roots in the early Pairpoint years when Pairpoint combined its wonderful silver-plated forms with Mount Washington Glass Company's beautiful glass. Popular through the first two to three decades of the twentieth century, its *old-fashioned* look was losing its appeal with the thoroughly-modern public as the 1920s came to a close. Initially, the glass components were clear/colorless relying on the beautiful engraved patterns to enhance the intricate metalwork, but as colored glass became popular in the 1920s, the metal forms were combined with cut or engraved colored glass. Although green was the most common color to be found on colored Fine Arts Line products, we regularly see lighting products that use Cobalt Blue, Canaria, and Auroria to create a lovely visual effect.

Pairpoint made it very easy to identify items from this product line. On every metal form they made, they permanently molded-in or die-stamped their signature and product identification number. There were literally hundreds of different styles and configurations offered within the Fine Arts Line, and examples appear regularly on the market. Quite often the silver plating or gold-wash on the metal components will be worn to the base metal and look rather shabby. These items can be replated quite easily, but be sure to use a reputable silversmith. (Refer to the *Support Services* chapter if you need a recommendation.) If you want to do some of the work yourself, the separation of the glass component from the metal is generally an easy task. Plaster of Paris is usually the setting compound used, and it will readily dissolve when submerged in water for a short time. When reassembling the metal and glass components, be sure to make-up a plaster putty to use as your setting material, and support the object until the plaster sets-up. DO NOT USE EPOXY or any other modern adhesive compounds or you will never be able to separate the pieces again without breaking them. ALWAYS REMEMBER when handling a Fine Arts Line item to lift it by the metal base. NEVER carry it by the glass top or insert; the plaster joint is the *weak link* and you may watch your metal base tumble to the floor and break.

The quality of the items from this product line is self-evident so expect to pay prices commensurate with that quality and level of detail.

A Fine Arts Line #4970 Cigarette Holder with the glass holder engraved in the English pattern. 7.25" h. $300.

Left and below:
A pair of Fine Arts Line C6147 Lamps with Green glass stems. The photograph below shows a detail view of the impressed signature found under the base. 12" to top of socket. $600/pair.

A Fine Arts Line Vase #C1510 with a Green glass insert engraved in the Brilliant pattern. 5.50" h. $350.

A Fine Arts Line #C6150 Lamp with a swirled green glass column. 12.50" to top of socket. $300.

A Fine Arts Line #4996 Cigarette Holder with a Clear glass insert engraved in the Mayfair pattern. 3.75" h. *From the collection of Craig and Christine Meraklis.* $250.

A Fine Arts Line 2-lite Mantel Lamp with a Bubble Ball connector and finial. 14" to top of finial. $400.

A Fine Arts Line #01570 Vase ensemble with the glass inserts engraved in the No.154 pattern. The impressed signature underneath identifies this item as being Pairpoint-Sheffield. $350.

A typical signature found impressed on items from the Fine Arts Line.

A label affixed to the bottom of a Fine Arts Line Lamp showing that Pairpoint applied, to many of their products, a clear protective lacquer coating to retard the silver plating from tarnishing. This feature probably occurred more frequently on those items that did not readily lend themselves to easy polishing.

Pewter Ware

Pairpoint was famous, and is well known today, for their high quality silver-plated table, personal, and decorative wares. However, very few collectors are aware that Pairpoint also produced a large product line of classically-styled decorative items made from pewter. The beauty of design and the quality of manufacture is superlative, yet the prices of items found today are very low. Unfortunately, and possibly a partial factor in the low pricing, most examples found will exhibit dents, bends, and general distortion of form. Pewter is a very soft metal and can be damaged very easily. Any reputable silversmith can restore your purchase to near-perfect condition for a price that will allow you to "remain in the ball game".

We recommend that you acquire a few examples of Pewter Ware for your collection. If you aren't familiar with your metallurgy, the product number stamped into the piece, along with the Pairpoint logo, will always be preceded by the letter "P" and include the word "PEWTER".

As strange as it may seem, you may find Pewter Ware that has been silver plated. These items, totalling 20 to 25 different forms, were made for the J. Diefendorf Company in the early 1930s. Some incorporated an engraved ship design. It is difficult to determine whether the base metal is pewter when the silver plating is intact. The item numbers are the same as the Pewter Ware designs, but instead of the prefix "P," a "B" or "C" was used. The use of the letter "C" on these is confusing, because many of the standard silver-plated wares used the letter "C" as the prefix to their catalog numbers.

A #P5575 Pewter Ware Pedestal Bowl. 8" d x 4.25" h. $150.

A #P1403 Pewter Ware Comport. 5.75" d x 8" h. $150.

A #P1515 Pewter Ware Vase. 6" h. $100.

An example of a typical impressed signature found on Pewter Ware items.

Tavern Glass

This line of products is particularly fascinating for several reasons. First, it is a departure from Pairpoint's formal style of glass-making to make a product line almost whimsical in nature. Second, with all the intentional flaws included within the glass, the pieces are of excellent workmanship and display all the features that have made Pairpoint products so well-regarded.

From information obtained from John Shuman's book, *American Art Glass*, page 45, the bubble effect in the glass was created by "the addition of potatoes to a batch of lime glass." From other long-since-forgotten sources, we remember reference being made to the insertion of willow branches into the molten glass batch to create the gas bubbles. Whichever technique was used by Pairpoint, the abundance of bubbles, and size variation, resulted in a unique effect. When one rubs one's hands and fingers over the glass surface, the lumps and bumps can be felt, and occasionally a sharp edge will be encountered where a bubble *popped* open.

The shapes found will be unique to Tavern Glass and the hand-applied, multi-colored enamel decoration is always present. Almost *cartoonish* in nature, the various decoration themes were generally figural. In addition to the Spanish Galleon, the Whale, the Basket of Flowers, the Rooster, and numerous other designs, scalloped edging and lines were applied using black enamel to trim-out the piece. All-in-all, a very nice effect!

Unlike every other glass line made by the Pairpoint Corporation, Tavern Glass was the one product line that was permanently marked in hand-painted enamel with a shape number and a decorating pattern number. You will find the form of the mark to be, for example, D1511/ 282, with the top number representing the shape and the bottom number representing the enameled design. Pairpoint made Tavern Glass in quite a few shapes, most of which are shown below, but don't be surprised to find a shape or enameled pattern that is different. We seriously doubt whether anyone would have difficulty identifying an example of Tavern Glass once they see the examples below and look for the identifying marks always present.

Tavern Glass is hard to find, more-so if you are geographically distanced from New England where the glass was made. The pieces you will find will most likely be pricey, but this line is likely to climb steadily in value.

A Tavern Glass #D1509 Vase with #282 Galleon enameled decoration, 5" h. $200.

A Tavern Glass #D1511 Vase with #282 Galleon enameled decoration, 8" h. $250.

A Tavern Glass #D1513 Vase with #285 Floral enameled decoration, 8" h. *Illustration from a Pairpoint Catalog.* $200.

A Tavern Glass Cordial with an unusual rooster and hen enameled decoration, 3.50" h. $75.

A detail view of the #281 Whale decoration. *Illustration from a Pairpoint Catalog.*

Venetti Design

The exquisite Venetti line has Venetian design influence and is usually the most expensive glass decorative line made by Pairpoint. Its unique shapes have classic beauty with wonderfully proportional balance. The glass is flawless and the red and white latticino twists are delicate and beautifully executed. The engraving design is unique to this line and of the finest quality; the cabochons are perfect little oval magnifying glasses. Finally, Venetti pieces are scarce; they fly off a dealer's shelf at almost any price faster than you can say "Venetti." If you can find it, buy it.

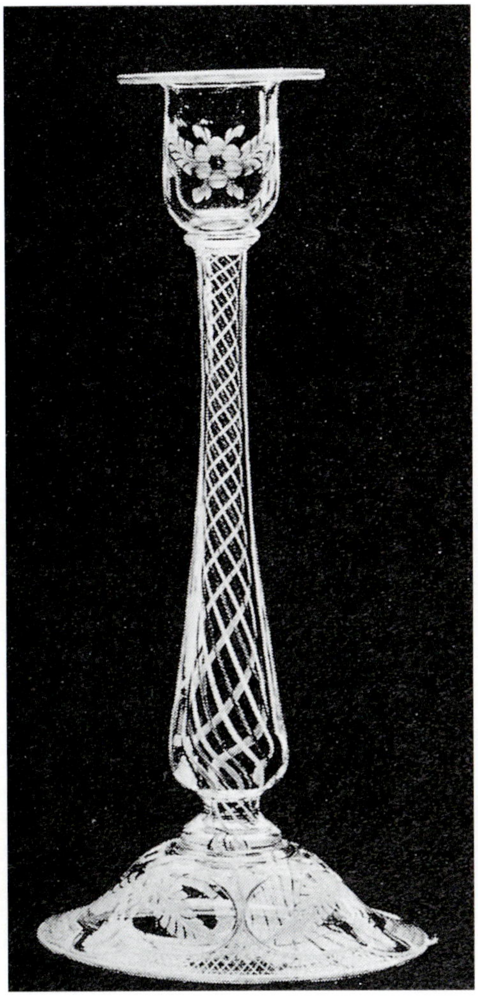

A Venetti #1810 Candlestick, 10" h. *Illustration from a Pairpoint Catalog.* $750.

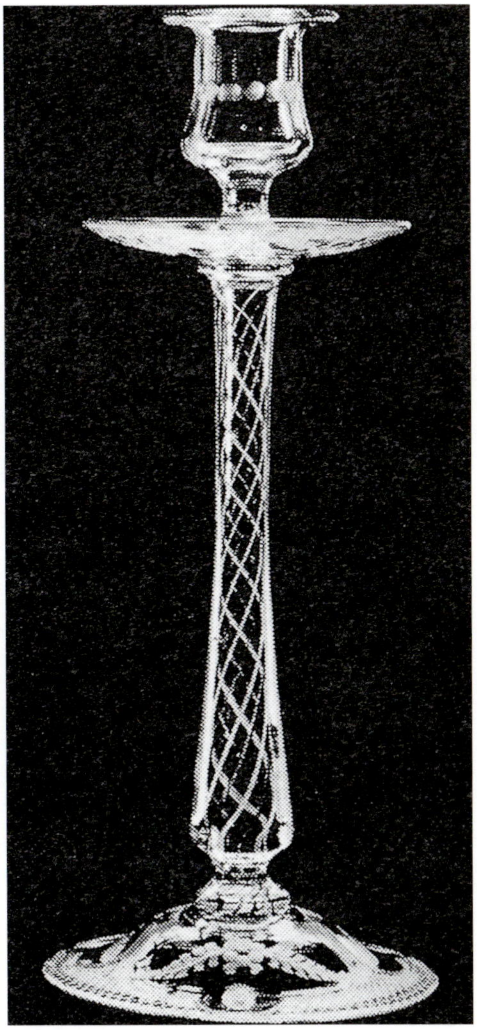

A Venetti #1811 Candlestick. *Illustration from a Pairpoint Catalog.* $750.

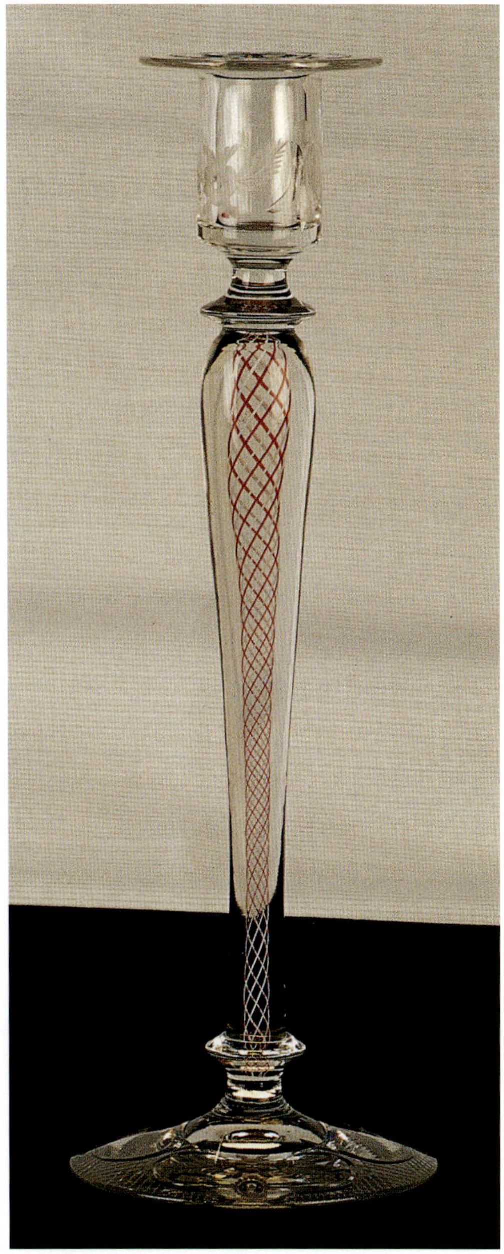

A Venetti #1812 Candlestick, (12" h), 14" h. $700.

A Venetti #1813 Candlestick. *Illustration from a Pairpoint Catalog*. $550.

A Venetti #1815 Comport, 8.75" d x 8.50" h. $900.

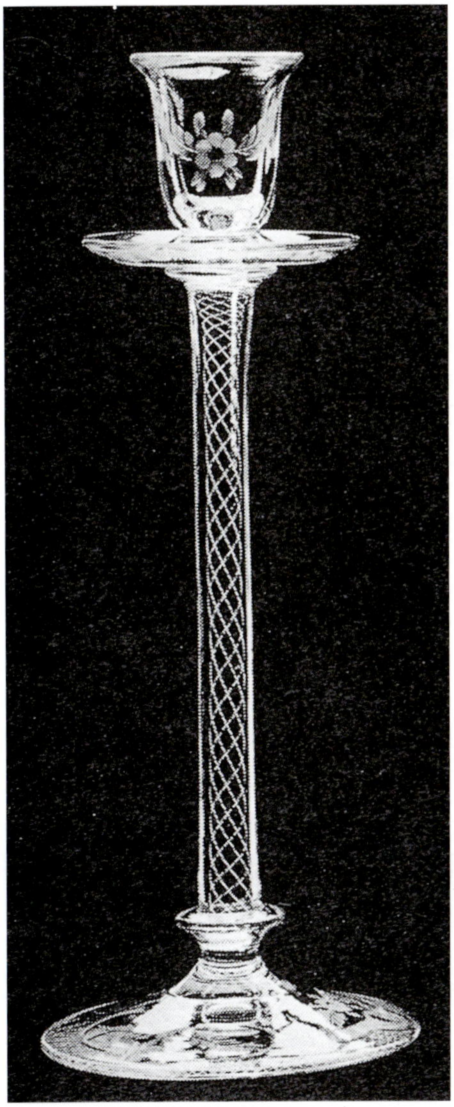

A Venetti #1814 Candlestick, 10" h. *Illustration from a Pairpoint Catalog.* $750.

A Venetti #1816 Comport, 8.25" d x 6.25" h. $1,200.

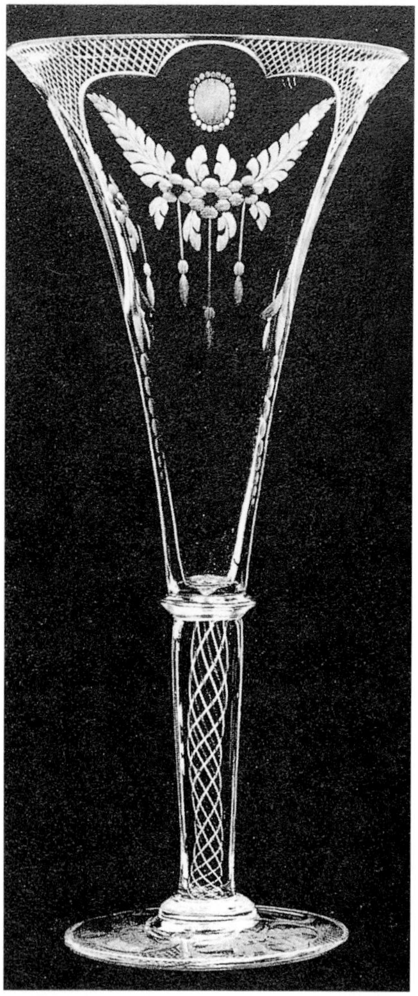

A Venetti #1817 Vase. *Illustration from a Pairpoint Catalog.* $1,200.

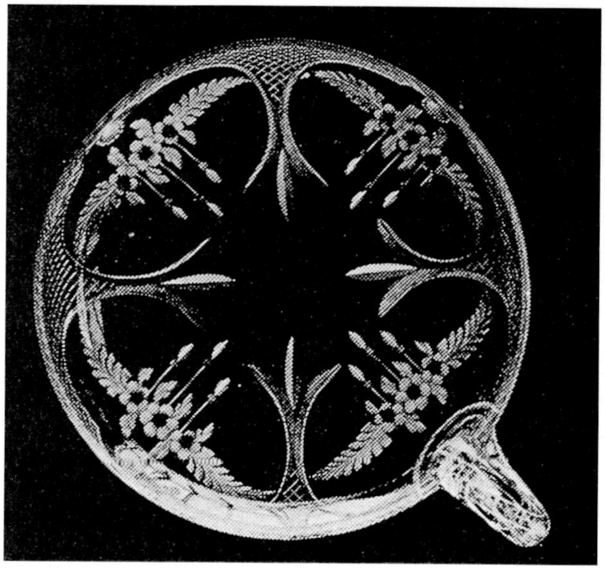

A Venetti #1819 Nappy. *Illustration from a Pairpoint Catalog.* $450.

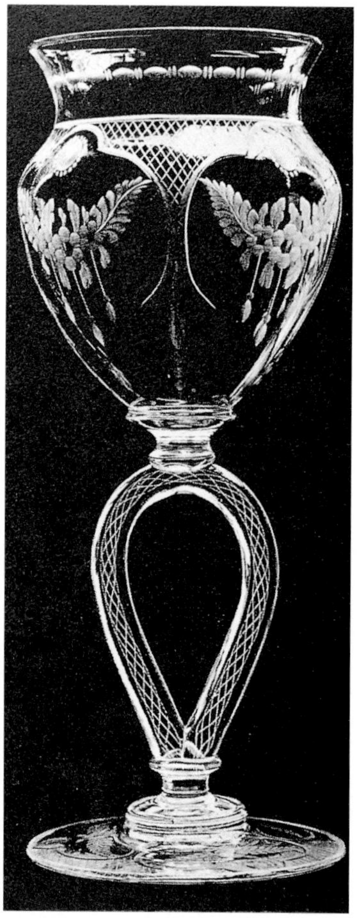

A Venetti #1818 Vase, 12" h. *Illustration from a Pairpoint Catalog.* $1,400.

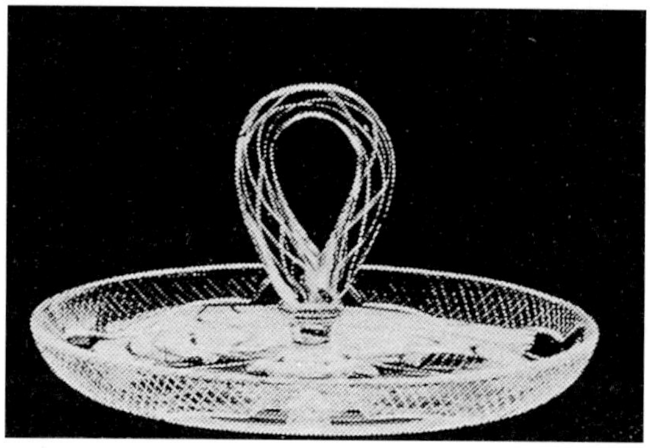

A Venetti #1820 Nappy. *Illustration from a Pairpoint Catalog.* $450.

A Venetti Footed Paperweight. $1,200.

A detail view of the engraving pattern that always appears on items from the Venetti line. Several years ago we observed a Venetti #1816 Comport that was missing the decoration but, of course, had the red/white air twist in the stem. We believe the piece was an unfinished example that somehow found its way out of the factory.

Chapter 6

Oddities

There are quite a few Pairpoint items that do not have a place anywhere else in this book, yet to exclude them would short-change the reader's overall sense of Pairpoint's significance in the market place. With this in mind, we have included items that may be of Pairpoint origin or are related to Pairpoint in some way, items that may provide a link to answering future questions. By thinking about them, your knowledge may be expanded. For example, if you find Pairpoint glass merged with sterling silver, is it an unauthorized, later marriage of broken components? We hope you enjoy the exercise.

An old "Bedford Glass, USA" label found in the boxes of Pairpoint documents salvaged from the factory ruins in the early 1960s by Charles Coulter. We have no idea at this time what this label may represent. *Courtesy of Charles and Barbara Coulter.*

A Pairpoint #18 silver plate and glass electrolier. This lamp is 18" high with the glass stem engraved in the No.154 pattern. $350/pair.

An example of the famous Pairpoint reverse-painted lamps that are so sought after today. 23" to top of shade. $7,500.

A real oddity...this is a dimensionally correct #B-228 Comport. Except for the bubble ball, this Comport has had its entire surface "frosted" in the same manner one would expect to find glass lamp shades or globes. We have never seen this type of surface treatment before on Pairpoint items, and are not quite certain what to make of it.

Opposite page:
These are pages from the 1937 printing of Neltje Blanchan's *The Bird Book*, originally copyrighted in 1897. The illustrations are a sampling of those created by Nellie (Ellen) M. Pairpoint, the daughter of Thomas J. Pairpoint, the namesake and first superintendent of the Pairpoint Manufacturing Co. She was born in 1865 and became a well-known illustrator of children's books and nature subjects.

THE BIRD BOOK

BIRD NEIGHBORS

BY

NELTJE BLANCHAN

With 32 Illustrations in Color and in Black and White by NELLIE M. PAIRPOINT

LITERARY GUILD OF AMERICA, INC.

MCMXXXVII NEW YORK

See page 41.

PURPLE MARTIN
(*Progne pubis*) Swallow family

See page 194.

THE AMERICAN ROBIN
(*Merula migratoria*) Thrush family

See page 187.

CARDINAL GROSBEAK
(*Cardinal cardinalis*) Finch family

A wonderful pair of custom-made Pairpoint #B-1617 Candlesticks modified and fitted to weighted sterling silver bases. To the surprise of many, these candlesticks are not a later "marriage of convenience", but were unquestionably intended to be a combination of materials. The proof is in the disassembly of the glass from the sterling base; the glass portion has a perfectly formed glass projection, approximately 1.50" long, coming from the bubble ball. The glass is set into the base using plaster-of-paris. This should silence the claim made by many that Pairpoint never fitted their glass to anything but plated silver. In addition to this example, we have personally seen three other examples of Pairpoint glass being legitimately merged with sterling silver. $1,600/pair.

An interesting example of a #B-1485 Vase. The color is a Teal Turquoise and the pontil mark has been left rough, but with a fire-polished finish to melt away the superficial roughness. The workmanship is excellent, the proportions are correct, but the variations in color, pontil finishing, and "ring" would indicate the time of manufacture to be post-Gundersen. $350.

A Rubber Rabbit Crib Toy, 7.75" h, with squeeker, manufactured by National Playthings, a division of The National Pairpoint Company, successor to the Gundersen Glass Works, Inc., upon the death of Robert Gundersen in 1952. $25-30.

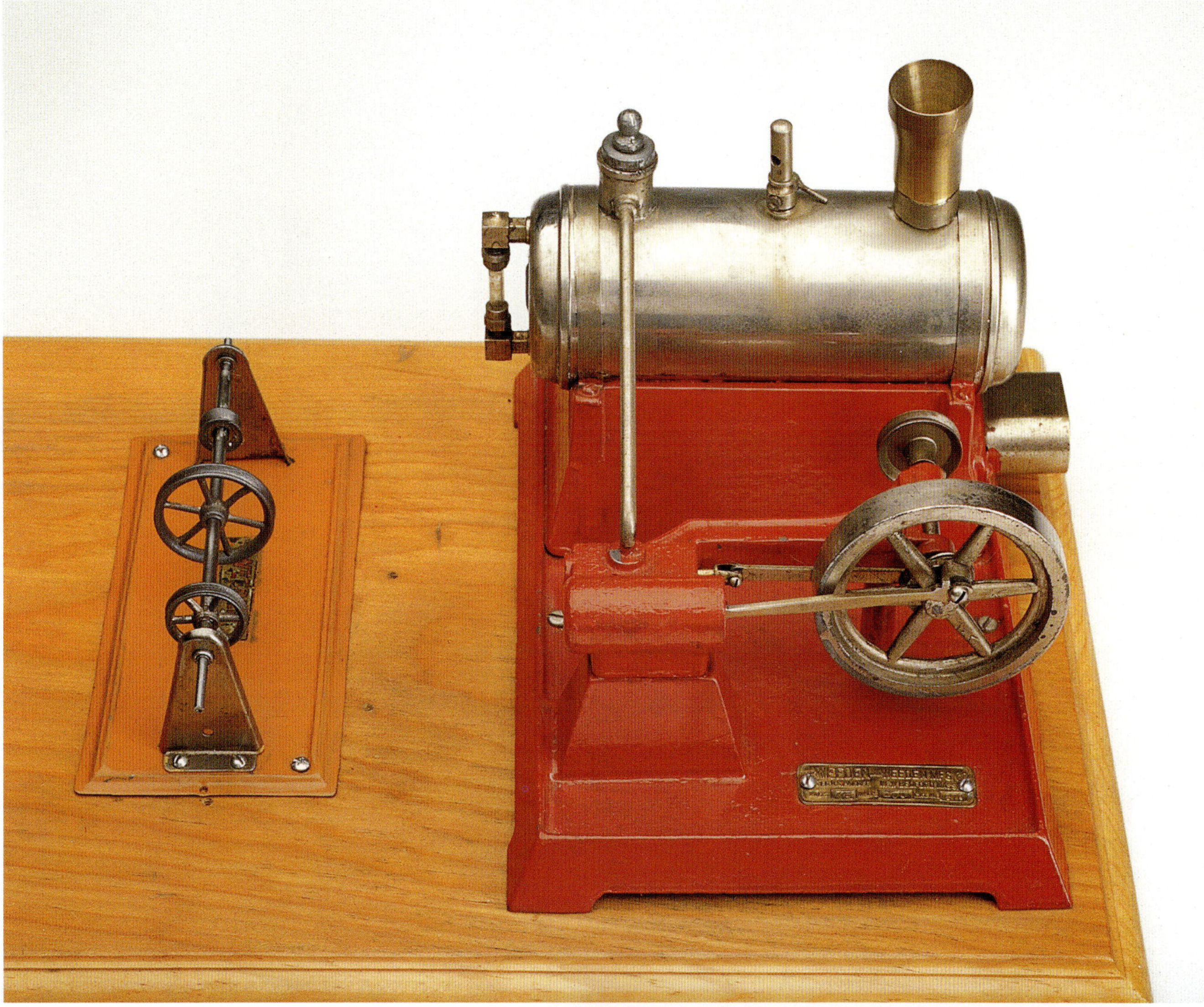

A WEEDEN STEAM ENGINE Model #670, with one accessory pulley shaft assembly, manufactured by National Playthings, a division of The National Pairpoint Company, which succeeded the Gundersen Glass Works, Inc. in 1952. $250-300.

An example of an Opal Bowl with Cobalt Blue spiraling stripes. 5" d x 4" h. This bowl was probably made under Robert Bryden's direction at the newly established East Wareham, Massachusetts plant during the latter part of 1957 until early 1958. This was Robert Bryden's first attempt at keeping the Pairpoint name alive after the New Bedford factory closed in the early part of 1957. This facility was closed in March of 1958, only five or six months after opening. $125.

A display of three Dresser Jars most likely produced from 1952-1957 by the Gundersen-Pairpoint Glass Works for Irving W. Rice & Co., New York. Left to Right $150, $250, $100 each.

A display of five different Perfume Bottles that represent the vast variety believed to have been produced for Irving W. Rice & Co., New York, during the Gundersen-Pairpoint years of 1952-1957. Left to Right $375, $325, $525, $325, $450 each.

This label and accompanying letter were discovered among the boxes of abandoned documents salvaged from the old factory in the years just prior to the devastating fire that finally removed all physical traces of Pairpoint's existence from New Bedford, Massachusetts. *Courtesy of Charles and Barbara Coulter.*

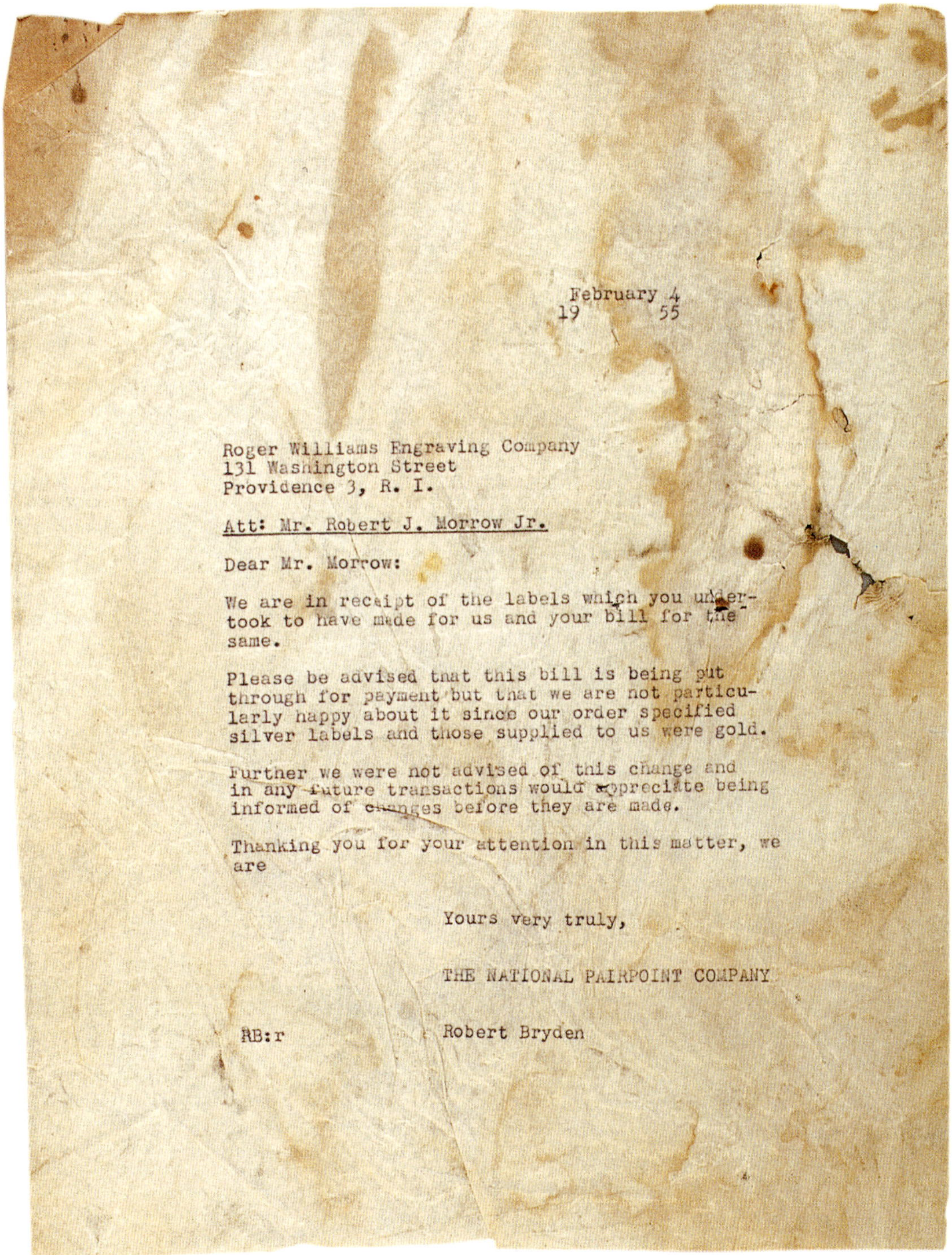

February 4
19 55

Roger Williams Engraving Company
131 Washington Street
Providence 3, R. I.

Att: Mr. Robert J. Morrow Jr.

Dear Mr. Morrow:

We are in receipt of the labels which you undertook to have made for us and your bill for the same.

Please be advised that this bill is being put through for payment but that we are not particularly happy about it since our order specified silver labels and those supplied to us were gold.

Further we were not advised of this change and in any future transactions would appreciate being informed of changes before they are made.

Thanking you for your attention in this matter, we are

Yours very truly,

THE NATIONAL PAIRPOINT COMPANY

RB:r Robert Bryden

The scarce limited edition (200) decorated Peach Blow Bell produced by Robert Bryden's Pairpoint Glass Company in 1973. An interesting feature of this particular bell is that it was decorated and signed by Cynthia Bryden, wife of Robert Bryden, who decorated for only a brief time in 1973. 12" high. $400.

A pair of decorated Peach Blow Candlesticks produced by Robert Bryden's Pairpoint Glass Company. They have the original paper label which identifies the place of manufacture as Sagamore, Massachusetts. 5.50" h. $300.

A small shiny Burmese creamer manufactured in Sagamore, Massachusetts by Robert Bryden's Pairpoint Glass Company around 1978. 3"h. Burmese pieces are much more scarce than Bryden's popular Peach Blow. $175.

A small Pitcher of Clear glass with Camellia spiral ribbing believed to have been produced during Robert Bryden's brief period in his East Wareham, Massachusetts factory during 1957 and 1958. $200.

The Paper Label used by Robert Bryden's Pairpoint Glass Company to identify glass items manufactured at his Sagamore, Massachusetts factory.

An example of an Amberina-type Goblet believed to be manufactured during either the Gundersen (1939-1952) or the Gundersen-Pairpoint (1952-1957) era, or later. (We have many original factory documents dating to these time periods that reference items identified as rose-amber.) There are small random bubbles throughout the glass. There is no pontil mark; the top edge has been finished by grinding. $175.

An example of the label being used on the Pairpoint glass being currently manufactured on Cape Cod.

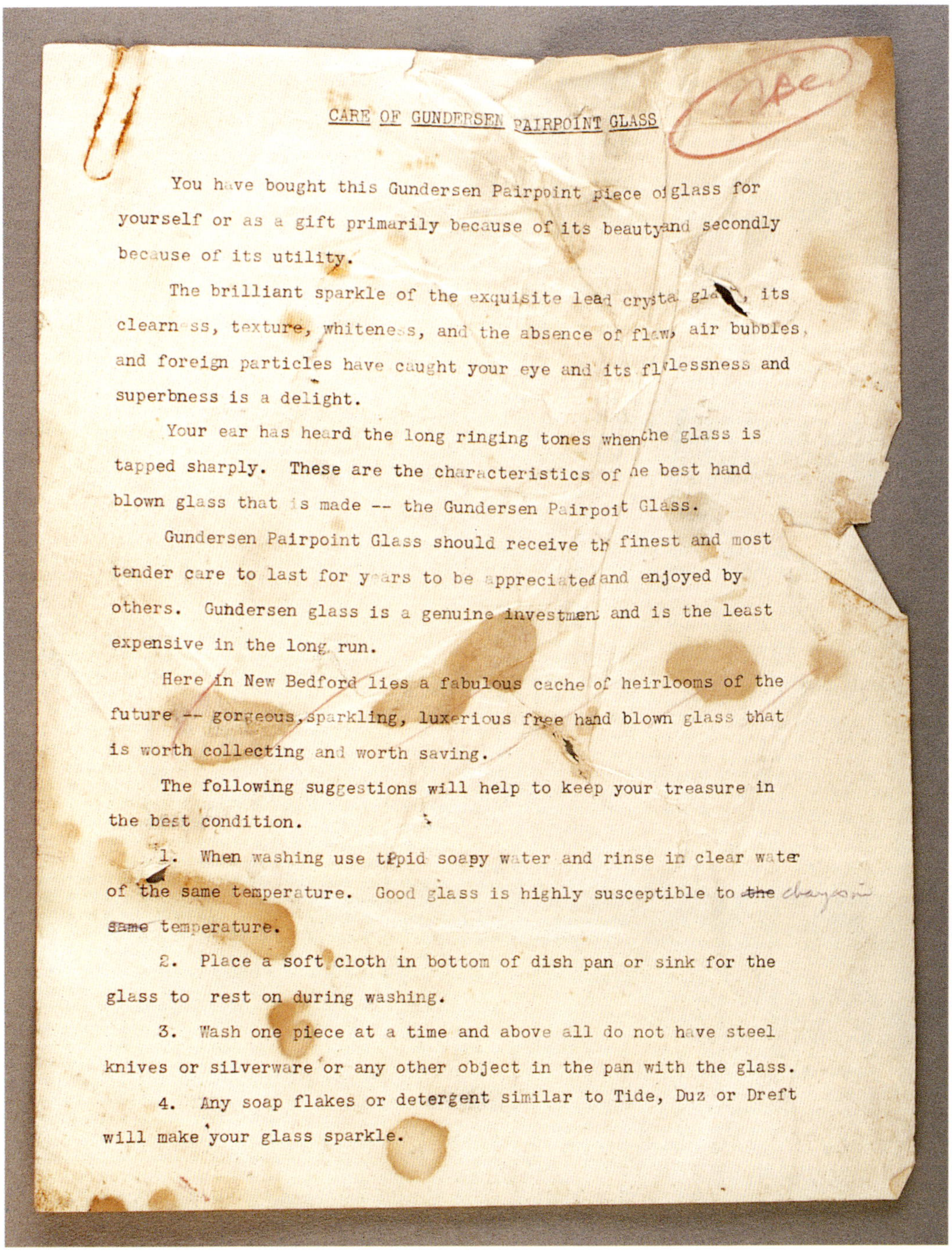

CARE OF GUNDERSEN PAIRPOINT GLASS

You have bought this Gundersen Pairpoint piece of glass for yourself or as a gift primarily because of its beauty and secondly because of its utility.

The brilliant sparkle of the exquisite lead crystal glass, its clearness, texture, whiteness, and the absence of flaws, air bubbles, and foreign particles have caught your eye and its flawlessness and superbness is a delight.

Your ear has heard the long ringing tones when the glass is tapped sharply. These are the characteristics of the best hand blown glass that is made -- the Gundersen Pairpoint Glass.

Gundersen Pairpoint Glass should receive the finest and most tender care to last for years to be appreciated and enjoyed by others. Gundersen glass is a genuine investment and is the least expensive in the long run.

Here in New Bedford lies a fabulous cache of heirlooms of the future -- gorgeous, sparkling, luxerious free hand blown glass that is worth collecting and worth saving.

The following suggestions will help to keep your treasure in the best condition.

1. When washing use tepid soapy water and rinse in clear water of the same temperature. Good glass is highly susceptible to ~~the same~~ changes in temperature.

2. Place a soft cloth in bottom of dish pan or sink for the glass to rest on during washing.

3. Wash one piece at a time and above all do not have steel knives or silverware or any other object in the pan with the glass.

4. Any soap flakes or detergent similar to Tide, Duz or Dreft will make your glass sparkle.

An interesting memorandum, found in the abandoned Pairpoint factory by Charles Coulter, that addresses the quality of the glass and the proper cautions that should be observed when cleaning and handling it. It is obvious from the text that the memo was written during the Gundersen-Pairpoint period, and from the chronological sequence of the old documents in our possession, we believe it dates to approximately 1954. *Courtesy of Charles and Barbara Coulter.*

Chapter 7
The Gundersen Years and Beyond

A Photo Essay

Robert Martinus Gundersen, glassblower extraordinaire for Pairpoint, was appointed Manager of the newly formed Gundersen Glass Works, Inc., in June of 1939. Pairpoint's assets had been purchased in 1938, by J&B Kenner, Inc., with the idea of continuing the operations of the now-defunct Pairpoint Corporation and capitalizing on the fine reputation always enjoyed by Pairpoint. Performance was essentially dysfunctional, and in early 1939, negotiations were conducted with Isaac N. Babbitt and Thomas Tripp, men of great integrity and experience in the glass and manufacturing fields, to re-purchase the assets and return Pairpoint to its previous levels of prosperity.

By combining the special talents of each of these three men, Gundersen Glass Works immediately undertook the task of reestablishing its customer network, currently in disarray, by continuing the production of standard Pairpoint-era products, as well as offering custom service to replace items damaged or lost by previous customers. Manufacturing quality remained high, and the wholesalers and general public were very satisfied with the products coming from Gundersen.

The period commencing at the end of World War II provided major challenges for Gundersen. The workers-of-old were essentially gone by now, new workers wanted no part of the made-by-hand glass industry, major foreign competition was only a couple years away, and consumers were demanding glass decorative items with more contemporary styling. Gundersen remained flexible and adapted well to the changing times. Many new products of high quality were introduced while special orders for the old Pairpoint product line were accepted. Absent during these years, however, was the proliferation of fine engraving work. Most of the experienced engravers were gone and, fortunately, the public preferred flowing free-form styles in the early 1950s. Even with the flexibility so well demonstrated by Gundersen for over ten years, the early 1950s brought the anguish of stiff competition from foreign glass makers who were introducing lower quality goods at much lower prices to the United States.

In 1952 the end of the Gundersen era was abruptly defined with the death of Robert Gundersen. The production of "Pairpoint" products continued with a partial degree of continuity for another five years until the factory had to be abandoned due to the poor condition of the machinery and structures. Since that time, and up to the present, Pairpoint's name has been kept alive by two more generations of fine glass artisans, the most notable being Robert Bryden. Pairpoint glass continues to be manufactured by hand today, honoring the memory of those who dedicated their lives to the production of some of the most beautiful glass in the world.

An original label, not often seen, used by the Gundersen Glass Works to identify their products. This label was found in the box of old documents salvaged from the abandoned New Bedford factory in the early 1960s by Charles Coulter. *Courtesy of Charles and Barbara Coulter.*

Right: The most commonly found label used by the Gundersen Glass Works to identify their products.

Although Gundersen continued the use of the famous bubble ball connector perfected by Pairpoint, they created their own swirl connector. The swirl connector was used in exactly the same way as the bubble ball, and it adorned many of Gundersen's designs.

A Gundersen Covered Urn with swirl connector and finial, 17" overall height. $800.

A very rare Gundersen Console Set in Ruby Red. The Ruby Red hollow ball connectors are particularly noteworthy. $1,500.

A small decorated Gundersen Burmese pitcher. Very little Burmese was made by Gundersen. 5.50" high. $400.

Examples of the types of Cornucopia Vases made during the Gundersen period. The vase on the left is in Marina Blue with a swirled foot. The vase on the right is in Ruby Red with a large, flattened bubble ball base. $200 each.

Opposite page:
A Ruby Red Gunderson Vase incorporating the swirl connector. In lieu of a colored foot, as would have been expected with Pairpoint, Gundersen quite regularly used Clear glass. $325.

A Gundersen #316 8-ounce Decanter with controlled bubbles throughout and a double optic. Original Gundersen Masterpiece label. $175.

A Gundersen Covered Comport, Rosaria, with a swirl connector and finial and a clear foot. $400.

A Gundersen Amethyst Comport with large bubble ball "paperweight" base. 7" d x 5.25" h. $225.

A short Ruby Red Gundersen Candlestick with a spiral connector and a clear foot. 4.75" h. $175.

A wonderful Ruby Red Gundersen Decanter with a bubble ball stopper. $275.

A # 4068 Gundersen Swan (12" long) in Rosaria. These are gracefully proportioned, especially in the way the beak follows the curve of the neck. The tip of the beak was intentionally ground in a vertical wedge and should not be mistaken as a repair. The Swans were made in a variety of sizes, and have been seen in Ruby Red, Marina Blue, Rosaria, Cobalt Blue, Camellia, and Clear. $600.

A Gundersen Comport in Marina Blue with a swirl connector at the top of the stem and a clear foot. 7.50" d x 6" h. $225.

Below:
A Gundersen free-form Vase in Ruby Red. 7" w x 10" l x 6.50" h. $300.

Appendix

Support Services

Damaged Pairpoint glass items are generally beyond salvage and should only be considered for purchase under very specific circumstances. However, there are two condition problems that we consider to be repairable, since no alteration or additional damage is required to return the item to its as-made condition. These include (1) the removal of the surface cloudiness found on *sick* glass (discussed in the Introduction) and (2) the restoration of the silver plating on items from the Fine Arts Line (discussed in Chapter 5). From our experience, we have come to trust the integrity and quality workmanship of the following companies when we needed repair services.

Sick Glass

Kim Carlisle & Associates, 28220 Lamong Road Dept. P, Sheridan, Indiana 46069. Telephone (317)758-5767. e-mail: kcarlisl@indy.net

"We clean cloudy glass — *Satisfaction Guaranteed.*" Kim Carlisle recommends a tumbling process instead of chemicals to remove the nasty deposits. This ensures a harder, smoother surface which will be less susceptible to future clouding. The process is definitely a repair as opposed to a treatment.

The process is very slow, so expect to have a couple months pass before receiving your item back. The results more than justify the wait. There aren't many bargains left in this world, but the cost to bring a cloudy piece of glass back to life is worthwhile.

Silversmith

Oexning Silversmiths-South, 320 Highway 197 South, Bakersville, North Carolina 28705. Telephone (828)688-9998. FAX (828)688-9976. Email: oexning@aol.com. Web Site: www.oxningsilversmiths.com. Ask for Elizabeth (Beth) Walker.

Don't go cheap when having your metalwork replated; you really will only get what you pay for. Beth Walker explained to me that there are basically two types of replating work being offered to the public. The lesser quality technique is to use nickel as the base layer and to flash over the nickel with a thin layer of silver. The nickel fills in a lot of surface irregularities, but also fills in much of the delicate design detail. Being naturally shiny, the nickel will disguise the thinness of the silver top layer. One of the down-side risks of this technique is that if your object is dropped by accident, the brittle nickel can crack and subsequently peel off. Solid silver plating remains very malleable and will usually flex with the base metal in the case of dropping or bending.

The better method is to plate only with solid silver to a thickness roughly equivalent to or thicker than the original triple or quadruple plating standard. This method is oriented toward the restoration of heirloom silver and silver-plate with a high degree of hand work.

Lacquering Silver

You may want to consider having your decorative silver items coated with clear lacquer. Pairpoint did use this technique to prevent the silver from tarnishing, so it would be legitimate for you to do the same. Although lacquering will retard tarnish for a long time, the trade-off for eliminating the need to polish will be the ever-so-slight loss of the sparkle of newly polished silver. The lacquer will not prevent tarnish forever, because, as hard as the lacquer finish may seem to be, the coating does *breathe* which allows oxygen to reach the surface of the silver. As time passes, you will detect a darkening of the surface, which usually occurs in spots. Polishing will not remedy the problem unless the lacquer is removed first.

Packing Glass

When shipping your glass, we can't over-stress the importance of packing your item correctly. Use a box that is slightly larger than your item. Wrap your item well using bubble wrap and/or peanuts, and be sure it is snug in the box. Then pack this small box into a larger box using tightly crumpled newspaper and peanuts as a buffer all around the small box. Seal the large box well, making sure the bottom is sealed as well as the top.

Bibliography

Avila, George C. *The Pairpoint Glass Story.* New Bedford, Massachusetts: George C. Avila and Reynolds-DeWalt Printing, Inc., 1968.

Blanchan, Neltje. *The Bird Book.* New York, New York: The Literary Guild of America, Inc., 1937. (Originally published by Doubleday, Doran & Company, Inc.)

Bredehoft, Neila. *The Collector's Encyclopedia of Heisey Glass 1925-1938.* Paducah, Kentucky: Collector Books, 1986.

Farrar, Estelle Sinclaire and Spillman, Jane Shadel *The Complete Cut & Engraved Glass of Corning.* New York, New York: Crown Publishers, Inc., 1979

Padgett, Leonard E. *Pairpoint Glass.* DesMoines, Iowa: Wallace-Homestead Book Co., 1979.

Shuman, John A. III. *The Collector's Encyclopedia of American Art Glass.* Paducah, Kentucky: Collector Books, 1988.

Index